thegoodwebguide

small businesses
and the self employed

annie ashworth

The Good Web Guide Limited • London

First Published in Great Britain in 2002 by The Good Web Guide Limited
Broadwall House, 21 Broadwall, London, SE1 9PL

www.thegoodwebguide.co.uk

Email:feedback@thegoodwebguide.co.uk

Original series concept by Steve Bailey

Cover photo ©

10 9 8 7 6 5 4 3 2 1

A catalogue record for this book is available from the British Library.

ISBN 1-903282-39-x

Project Editor Michelle Clare

Design by Myriad Creative Ltd

Printed in Italy at LEGO S.p.A.

dedication

To Tom, Louis and Toby and to Mark the Iron(ing) Man
for letting me get on with it.

contents

the good web guides

The World Wide Web is a vast resource, with millions of sites on every conceivable subject. There are people who have made it their mission to surf the net: cyber-communities have grown, and people have formed relationships and even married on the net.

However, the reality for most people is that they don't have the time or inclination to surf the net for hours on end. Busy people want to use the internet for quick access to information. You don't have to spend hours on the internet looking for answers to your questions and you don't have to be an accomplished net surfer or cyber wizard to get the most out of the web. It can be a quick and useful resource if you are looking for specific information.

The Good Web Guides have been published with this in mind. To give you a head start in your search, our researchers have looked at hundreds of sites and what you will find in the Good Web Guides is a collection of reviews of the best we've found.

The Good Web Guide recommendation is impartial and all the sites have been visited several times. Reviews are focused on the website and what it sets out to do, rather than an endorsement of a company, or their product. A small but beautiful site run by a one-man band may be rated higher than an ambitious but flawed site run by a mighty organisation.

Relevance to the UK-based visitor is also given a high premium: tantalising as it is to read about purchases you can make in California, because of delivery charges, import duties and controls it may not be as useful as a local site.

Our reviewers considered a number of questions when reviewing the sites, such as: How quickly do the sites and individual pages download? Can you move around the site easily and get back to where you started, and do the links work? Is the information up to date and accurate? And is the site pleasing to the eye and easy to read? More importantly, we also asked whether the site has something distinctive to offer, whether it be entertainment, inspiration or pure information. On the basis of the answers to these questions sites are given ratings out of five. As we aim only to include sites that we feel are of serious interest, there are very few low-rated sites.

Bear in mind that the collection of reviews you see here are just a snapshot of the sites at a particular time. The process of choosing and writing about sites is rather like painting the Forth Bridge: as each section appears complete, new sites are launched and others are modified. If you register at the Good Web Guide site you can check out the reviews of new sites and updates of existing ones, or even have them emailed to you.

By registering at our site, you'll find hot links to all the sites listed, so you can just click and go without needing to type the addresses accurately into your browser.

All our sites have been reviewed by the author and research team, but we'd like to know what you think. Contact us via the website or email feedback@thegoodwebguide.co.uk. You are welcome to recommend sites, quibble about the ratings, point out changes and inaccuracies or suggest new features to assess.

You can find us at www.thegoodwebguide.co.uk

user key

 £   Subscription

 R   Registration Required

     Secure Online Ordering

 UK   Country of Origin

introduction

'To open a business is easy. To keep it open is very difficult.'
Chinese proverb

'Entrepreneurship is the last refuge of the troublemaking individual.'
James Glassman

To understand the importance of small business in this county, it's worth looking at the most recent statistics:

• In the first six months of 2001, 189,570 new business started up in England and Wales, and 203,180 closed.
• In a Spring 2001 survey by Barclays Bank, three per cent of the adult population of England and Wales were in the process of starting a new business.

Currently there are:
• Around 3.7 million active businesses in the UK
• Of that figure only 25,000 are medium sized (with 50-249 employees) and 7000 are classed as large (with 250 plus employees)
• Small businesses, including those without employees, account for over 99 per cent of all businesses, with 37% of the entire annual turnover.
• Out of 3.7 million businesses, 2.6m are sole proprietors.
• The greatest area of business growth in the last five years has been amongst 'Micro' businesses, employing less than 10 people
• 2 million of the 3.7 million active businesses have a turnover of less than £50,000 (the VAT paying threshold).

[Source: Small Business Service www.sbs.gov.uk]

It's plain to see that small businesses are a vital part of the economy, and no wonder then that there is so much information available for then on the Internet. In fact, it's arguable that there are more resources available on the Internet than can be found anywhere else. The world-wide web is an important, if not an essential, element in running a small business at the start of the twenty first century.

Whether you have the germ of a business idea, have been running an enterprise successfully for a while and need finance to expand, or whether you are an established business who needs to keep abreast of regulations and business trends, the information is at your fingertips, and there in abundance.

For this reason, access to the Internet should be at the core of every small business person's armoury. And as our links with Europe become ever closer, and membership of the Euro looks more than likely, small businesses will need to keep abreast of regulations from Brussels. The Internet has an important role to play here as a resource for up-to-the-minute information.

Critical too is the role business to business websites have in connecting the people who earn their living from home or small offices. Guidance and mentoring, financial and legal advice, products like insurance to buy online are all making the home-based office a very viable place to earn your living.

Financial planning is even possible to control remotely. Pensions can be compared and brought online, business travel's itineraries sorted and tickets bought, and larger operations can even organise their payroll, invoicing and credit control exclusively through the Internet.

The banks have a particular relevance here. As they become less and less customer friendly on the high street, with branches closing or becoming automatic teller lobbies only, the banks are offering a feast to their customers through internet banking facilities, loan offers and advice online. The bank sites we reviewed were impressive; each one has a section aimed at the small business account and they are in a head to head battle with each other to lure your custom.

The Government too has been quick to grasp the potential of the web. The Department of Trade and Industry especially has spread its net far and wide, and with a government department exclusively interested in the concerns of small business, the future is looking bright. Taxation too has taken a firm hold of the advantages of cyberspace, and with the possibility now of completing income tax returns and VAT returns online, time-consuming paperwork can be cut to the minimum.

The websites we found least inspiring were those concerned with marketing, or at least marketing offline. Of course the Internet itself has become the new advertising vehicle, and there is much to be found online about the beneficial impact a presence on the web can have on your business. Ironically there are lessons to be learned from the websites in this book about what works and what doesn't. The web gives you an unprecedented opportunity to log on to a competitor's site, to see what they are up to, and to steal a march on them.

To keep the depressing news until last: though over 400,000 business may have started up in 2000, 397,000 failed or closed for one reason or another. Reason enough to use every resource available to keep your head above water. May this book be invaluable to you, and help your business, however ambitious, to fulfil its potential.

Annie Ashworth
March 2002

pick of the best

Sites deserving a special mention:

www.acas.org.uk
Advisory, Conciliation and Arbitration Service

www.smallbusiness.barclays.co.uk
Barclays Bank Business Banking

www.british-franchising.org
British Franchising Association

www.anewbusiness.co.uk
Business Group Plc

www.thebiz.co.uk
Business Information Zone

www.businesslink.org
Business Link

www.businesstraveller.com
Business Traveller

www.compactlaw.co.uk
CompactLaw

www.ednet-ni.com
The Economic Development Network for Northern Ireland

www.freelawyer.co.uk
Free Lawyer

www.homeworking.com

Homeworking

www.legal-advice-online.co.uk
Legal Advice Online

www.natwest.com
NatWest

www.scottishbusinesswomen.co.uk
Scottish Business Women

www.smallbusinessadvice.org.uk
Small Business Advice

www.startups.co.uk
Startups

www.trainingzone.co.uk
Training Zone

Chapter 01

Essential Sites

It would take the most determined and conscientious entrepreneur to wade through the vast array of websites offering advice and information for small businesses, but we have called these sites essential because they look at business activity in the broadest sense.

Running an enterprise alone, or with just a partner, can be lonely, especially if you are at the start-up stage with the germ of an idea, but are at a loss to know what happens next. These sites are designed for those whose qualifications may not include a degree in business studies, and most will lead you through the maze of business registration, employment and taxation issues. Some offer you access to professional advisers online and most provide excellent links to other sites that can answer your specific business questions. There is plenty here too for businesses that are well underway, but need to grow or change direction. Best of all, much of the advice comes from sources with impressive credentials, and most of it is free.

general sites

www.anewbusiness.co.uk
Business Group Plc

Overall rating: ★ ★ ★ ★ ★			
Classification:	information	**Readability:**	★ ★ ★ ★
Updating:	regularly	**Content:**	★ ★ ★ ★ ★
Navigation:	★ ★ ★ ★	**Speed:**	★ ★ ★ ★

UK   R

A very straight forward idea from the Birmingham based, Business Group Plc, which provides new business with an instant company name and domain name search facility.It has access to over two million businesses and one million companies, and is split into four sections covering information about Business Group Plc, Nationwide Corporate Services (which can help you form a UK or offshore company), Business Names Registration (with instant availability check and application forms), and Nationwide Trade Marks (listed by class and alphabetically).

SPECIAL FEATURES

Business Group Plc has a registration service for an annual fee, and outlines the benefits of different types of companies (Ltd, Plc, partnership and so on).

The Business tips are some of the best around, with 50 sensible ideas and points to check.

Once you know what it is you want to sell, this site should be your first stop. Time saving with sensible advice. Premier league.

www.bizzadvice.com
Bizz Advice

Overall rating: ★ ★ ★ ★			
Classification:	information	**Readability:**	★ ★ ★ ★ ★
Updating:	regularly	**Content:**	★ ★ ★ ★ ★
Navigation:	★ ★ ★ ★	**Speed:**	★ ★ ★ ★

UK   R   £   🔒

When so much information is available free online, one wonders what the point of a website is where 'members' have to pay for advice. But BizzAdvice's explanation is that it gives access to a variety of business experts in a variety of fields who can give you direct answers to your specific questions.

BizzAdvice claims the advantage of being a pan-European information marketplace for start-ups or growing businesses, connecting people 'in need of information and advice with people who have the knowledge and background to help others become successful'. The team is certainly impressive, with a combination of Internet entrepreneurs, experienced consultants, financiers and venture capitalists. The promotional blurb refers to the company's 'extensive knowledge and experience in Entrepreneurship, Technology, E-commerce, Finance and Management Consulting', but loses marks for remaining enigmatic and anonymous. Why should one have to dig though a website to find out the names behind it? However, they boast backgrounds in an array of management consultancy firms and blue chip companies. As MD or tea lady one wonders?

How does it work?

Members – who join free – can sign in and ask an adviser directly by selecting a category which relates to the question they want to ask, then select an adviser from the list offered.

The advisers (individuals as well as organisations) have a list of the number of questions asked next to their name, as well as a star rating, given by members who have posed questions. Once you have chosen your adviser, you indicate the amount you want to pay, or have the option to leave this space clear for the adviser to suggest a price.

Questions can also be asked publicly, and advisors will bid to answer. Either way, your response will be emailed back to you, with a hyperlink to your answer. On receipt of it, your credit card will be debited for the agreed amount. Simple, isn't it?

BizzAdvice stresses it is a secure site, and there is a 14 day money back guarantee if you feel your query has not been dealt with adequately.

Subjects covered include accounting, finance, legal, start-up, technology, e-commerce, human resources, marketing, tax, and others covering import/export, writing and editing, translation and real estate. Within each subject there might be 10 or so advisors, some having been asked over 100 questions, some none, and the fees vary from a free initial consultation to £400 per day. One adviser is profiled and highlighted on the homepage.

Call us cynical, but it would take the brave to agree a fee for information they have not yet received, and over the net. The most valuable part of the site, to our mind, is the Start-up information, which covers business plan basics, registering your business, finance, recruitment, marketing, and trading over the Internet. With each section there is well-written, helpful advice, and further links to more detailed information. The site links too are good, and feature old favourites like the British Chamber of Commerce, BVCA, Companies House, DTI, NBAN amongst others.

SPECIAL FEATURES

Hot Topic is changed regularly, but small features on Stakeholder pensions and the Data Protection Act, take you to the advisers; in other words you have to pay if you want to know more.

Directory is actually a link to The Business Information Zone (see p.73 for a review), where you can click on categories of interest. To review questions up for bid, there is an index of queries pending, and the bids received.

Forum includes a chat room, jobs section, office space availability and your own products and services promotion facility.

Business advice facility for the Brave New World, and for those brave enough to take the plunge. The way to go for online advice, so long as the questions you pose are as detailed as possible to ensure you receive the best possible advice for the fee you are paying. The adviser profiles are good, and the back-up behind the site seems reliable.

www.bizwise.co.uk
Bizwise

Overall rating: ★ ★ ★ ★			
Classification:	information	**Readability:**	★ ★ ★ ★
Updating:	regularly	**Content:**	★ ★ ★ ★
Navigation:	★ ★ ★ ★	**Speed:**	★ ★ ★ ★

UK   R   £   🔒

Bizwise claims to be a portal website for SMEs, without the 'annoying banners'. Its aim is to provide sound advice and resources for new and existing businesses in a no-nonsense format. There is guidance on finance, employment, law, regulations and more, all free (though certain information has to be paid for and readers are requested to log on to access some of the articles). The style is certainly clear and definitely comprehensive, with a home page scattered with articles, links and indexing.

SPECIAL FEATURES

Newsfeed provides features on current issues in the press. Highlighted on the home page is a selection of articles provided by professional firms specialising in a particular field, and many here are news sensitive too. However, the Business Advice Search is a short cut to the information within the whole site. A request for details of the Companies Act resulted in a selection of articles, though nothing came up for PAYE.

New features include Internet, Finance and Legal Advice, with each one providing decent-sized articles on subjects including web features, slow payment, business start up planning, part-time work, and staff employment regulations amongst many others. Each section has a facility for finding a specialist adviser locally, regionally or nationally. There are links to website designers and a lengthy choice of legal documents from the Law Docs service, which can be downloaded to your PC. Some of these need to be paid for by an online secure payment scheme.

Find an Adviser covers a vast array of specialists including the ubiquitous lawyers and accountants (a postcode search yielded six pages of these in the SW17 area alone) as well as consultants, creative writers, debt recovery and that's only as far as D alphabetically!) The addresses are displayed free, and you log on for more information. The opportunity is there too to add your own companies details under Add Your Business.

Official Publications (from Horse's Mouth) cover official documents and government publications from bodies such as HM Customs and Excise and the Inland Revenue, and produced three pages of options on a Corporation Tax search.

Events covered include seminars, exhibitions and training courses, though this facility is date sensitive.

OTHER FEATURES

There is a Paymentor link (for debt collection); a search engine submission facility (in association with Bpath); a company formation service (Bizwise can set up the whole company for you including buying off-the-shelf companies). There is a list of FAQs and company names currently available; company and director reports; financial reports online and a marketing list service.

Bizwise promises much and delivers plenty. The beauty of this site is that it can help the green entrepreneur, but there is plenty of advice and resources for the more established ones.

www.clearlybusiness.com
Clearly Business

Overall rating: ★ ★ ★			
Classification:	information	**Readability:**	★ ★ ★ ★
Updating:	regularly	**Content:**	★ ★ ★ ★
Navigation:	★ ★ ★	**Speed:**	★ ★ ★ ★

UK

When will website designers learn that there is beauty in simplicity? Clearly Business, the business site owned 60% by Freeserve and 40% by Barclays Bank, claims to be entirely independent and it has left no stone unturned in its aim to be both a comprehensive resource and effective portal site, and frankly the result is terrifying.

The site boasts 20 channels, from accounting and tax, through communications, building a website, computing, credit management, HR, legal services, to utilities, and each one features articles relevant to that subject. Start-up has lightly written summaries of the basic considerations before launching into business, and then has Services and Guides links from registering your company online to the beginners guide to contracts.

With at least 60 links on the homepage, it's enough to make a busy entrepreneur throw their hands up in horror, but persevere if you can bear to. Once you have decided what it is you want to research, the information is there in spadefuls, with no end of features on a variety of topics and links to relevant websites. Not advisable for those starting out. Though the information is available, you may be overwhelmed by the sheer volume of information, so look elsewhere first if your confidence is at a low ebb.

To keep life simple, tabs along the home page are labelled Your Business, Your eBusiness, Your Finances and Your Community, and short drop down menus list the major subjects in each area.

SPECIAL FEATURES

Finances covers accounting and tax, banking and raising finance, insurance, and credit management. These links take you straight to relevant features and are the quickest way of navigating the site.

The centre panel gives teasers about highlights within the site, including a chat forum and poll facility, current affairs issues, news and analysis.

Links are packed in – and are direct from the homepage – to business resources, broadly listed under Information and Products (Datamonitor Research, Eversheds Debt Recovery etc), Services (Legal services insurance online etc), Internet and Telephony (domain names, web design, search engine registration etc).

OTHER FEATURES

Delve into yet more boxed links to find equipment auctions, Insight (a regular roundup publication of the latest news and information), an Online Business Service for managing your books, Free Market Research (accessing Datamonitor), Business Documents (with standard letter templates) and the latest communication hardware (fax machines, mobile phones and telecommunications equipment).

Freeserve have pulled out all the stops here to promote the fantastic potential of the Internet. The bonuses of the Clearly Business site are in the quantity of information, but to be negative it has become carried away with its own cleverness. Information about the aims of the site would be better outlined right from the word go, with basic links to subjects. As it stands it's a muddle. Not for the faint hearted.

www.credit-to-cash.com
Credit to Cash

Overall rating: ★ ★ ★ ★			
Classification:	information	**Readability:**	★ ★ ★ ★ ★
Updating:	weekly	**Content:**	★ ★ ★
Navigation:	★ ★ ★ ★	**Speed:**	★ ★ ★ ★ ★

UK US

This site is run by ROK Associates Credit & Debt Management Limited and regulated by the Office of Fair Trading and is jam-packed with business information. It calls itself the small business portal, but is more than just links to other relevant sites. There are articles on all areas of small business, including start-up, financing, franchising, debt recovery and cash flow control. Under Business Banking, there is a no-holds-barred review of the banking websites, with links to the main banks offering financial services for businesses. The Articles Database will remove the need to negotiate the rather overwhelming homepage.

SPECIAL FEATURES

Newsletter Email your details and you'll receive a weekly newsletter that includes new articles and a Q & A forum.

Favorite (sic) pages are highlighted on the homepage and throughout the site. They include samples of business plans, advice on marketing a small business and FAQs on National Insurance and Self-Assessment (with links to the Inland Revenue).

Articles cover the whole of the UK, so small businesses in Scotland for example can access a rich vein of Scottish sites.

Downloads include free software (in UK pound, US dollar and world versions) and forms on over 40 subjects.

New Bank Account facility enables those who are UK resident and want a personal or business bank account, but have too poor a credit rating (resulting from County Court Judgements/ defaults/bankruptcy/voluntary arrangements/liquidation), to open an account with a 'high street' bank.

The Business Insurance page has advice on trade and credit insurance and excellent company insurance tips, plus links to Royal Bank of Scotland and HSBC. There are recommended books, and an index of details on the rest of the site. Click on your area of interest under Small Business Accounting, and a service provider affiliated to the site will contact you directly.

The Company Doctor is a free business advice service, and debt mediation service, with examples of companies helped by ROK Associates.

A useful site in the breadth of ground it covers, but something doesn't smell quite right. A good resource for information, but faceless. Who is the company behind the website and who are these companies offering free advice?

www.fsb.org.uk
Federation of Small Business

Overall rating: ★ ★ ★ ★			
Classification: information		**Readability:**	★★★★
Updating: occasionally		**Content:**	★★★★
Navigation: ★★★		**Speed:**	★★★★

UK

The FSB is the UK's largest Small Business Lobby Group, set up nearly 30 years ago, and the website is comprehensive, though at times a little hard to navigate. The FSB's enthusiasm is almost tangible, but at the cost of clarity. Though much of the site is free to browsers, with information on setting up your own business in a broad sense, the thrust is really in the FSB's work lobbying the government to get fair treatment for small business owners and the self-employed. By joining, members can get privileges including financial help with the legal and accountancy costs of an Inland Revenue or VAT investigation, PAYE disputes, Data Protection issues, or employment disputes. Membership also includes savings on insurance, phone bills, internet access and so on.

SPECIAL FEATURES

National News page with up-to-date news updates on the activities of the FSB.

Newsletter comes free by email, from the Federation.

Features on current political issues, such as legislation updates or the impact of fuel taxes, with links to regional information in detail.

Links to useful sites and free software downloads including Acrobat Reader and Excel Reader.

FSB Extras covers information and activities, such as seminars from which members and non-members can benefit.

The site will be of particular interest to small business owners with a political inclination who want to have a voice in lobbying Parliament on SME issues.

www.nfea.com
National Federation of Enterprise Agencies

Overall rating: ★ ★ ★ ★			
Classification: information		**Readability:**	★ ★ ★ ★
Updating: sporadically		**Content:**	★ ★ ★ ★
Navigation: ★ ★ ★ ★		**Speed:**	★ ★ ★
UK			

A slightly different ballgame to its sister site www.smallbusinessadvice.org.uk (see p.22), which is well-written and informative. This one is harder to read, but worth persevering with if you are looking for information on Local Enterprise Agencies (LEAs) in your area.

Not to be confused with the government's education department, LEAs are limited companies, made up of partnerships between the private sector and local authorities. They are valuable to small businesses as a resource for advice and support, counselling and training. The Nfea brings them all together and works as voice for influencing government, the EU and other key decision makers to create favourable conditions for small businesses.

SPECIAL FEATURES

Click on the map to find your nearest LEA. Catch up on the Nfea's activities, and find out how to become involved in the pilot scheme, The Business Volunteers Mentors Association.

Download PDF files of the Nfea's annual reports and press releases, though under Documents for Discussion there was silence! The links are good, and not surprisingly the same as those in smallbusinessadvice.org.uk.

A useful resource if you require information about Local Enterprise Agencies.

www.sfedi.co.uk
Small Firms Enterprise Development Initiative

Overall rating: ★ ★ ★			
Classification: information		**Readability:**	★ ★
Updating: sporadically		**Content:**	★ ★ ★ ★ ★
Navigation: ★ ★ ★		**Speed:**	★ ★ ★ ★ ★
UK			

This is the website of the government appointed agency 'to identify standards of best practice for small business'. Not surprisingly there is little that is cosy about it: written in the business jargon which can only come from a government agency, it can take a while to get into the swing of the language. However, the Sfedi's heart is in the right place, even if it does rather pompously express its intentions to deliver 'the highest standards of small business support provision'.

For all that, the site is an excellent reference source and access point for enormous resources and advice for new businesses and existing ones wanting support. The Sfedi's 'Team' of business advisors don't look exactly chummy, but professional and comfortingly reliable. Features include a list of products which carry the Sfedi's stamp of approval and which can be bought or linked to online. There's a free newsletter to which can be emailed to your desk, but alarmingly the Stop Press news was horribly out of date.

SPECIAL FEATURES

Pre-Start outlines a Sfedi's project to identify people's competence to work for themselves. The Consultation facility enables the potentially self-employed to receive information by email.

Start up gives a 'standards overview', which, in layman's terms, is a checklist for those wanting to set up their own enterprise. Click down subjects on the Standards Overview to help prepare a business plan and to make sure there is no area of the enterprise which has not been thought through. There's a selection of case studies (with glowing testimonials of the Sfedi's assistance), and a link to the products catalogue. There's also a link to www.startups.co.uk (see p.23).

Existing Business links to www.homebusiness.org.uk (see p.28) and outlines Sfedi's supprt documents for those wanting to improve their business potential. Pages here include staff issues and health and safety, with a checklist as for Start up, and a link to the products catalogue.

Business Support covers standards for business survival, and includes advice, a Standards Overview with reminders on handling a client relationship ('help monitor and improve services' or 'give feedback to clients'), and links to the product catalogue.

Design spells out simply the various areas of design and its importance in business presentation. To the uninitiated job roles amongst the design team are explained and standards of good practice explained.

Research gives free access to the Sfedi's research documents online, such as the Impact of Training on Small Firms and Products is Sdefi's catalogue, including books, training programmes and qualifications, all endorsed, and details of how to apply for an endorsement.

The advantages of this site is that it is well-intentioned, with reliable information and support service, and excellent links to a good small business support service. It could however do with a good shake up.

www.smallbiz.uk.com
Smallbiz

Overall rating: ★ ★ ★ ★			
Classification:	information	**Readability:**	★ ★ ★ ★
Updating:	daily	**Content:**	★ ★ ★ ★
Navigation:	★ ★ ★ ★ ★	**Speed:**	★ ★ ★ ★
UK			

Smallbiz is a portal site to other websites that are useful to small businesses and entrepreneurs. The site claims to be quick and easy, and what you see is what you get, so you can find out what you need to know fast.

There are eleven sections in the index, each one containing seven items listed down the left hand side of the page. The pop-up menu on the home page allows you to register for the Smallbiz newsletter, and within Smallbizcentre, businesses can promote their own websites in the Smallbiz webstreet, or join the email discussion group.

SPECIAL FEATURES

The Business Directory is truly awe inspiring, with over 1.8 million UK businesses listed. A search by postcode for stationery suppliers in one locality threw up over 30 entries, including the local village post office.

Smallbiz Plus links to online researchers, Virtual File safe and Alldaypa.com (the 24hr secretary and admin resource site). Staff and Skills has useful links to OneclickHR for pay and benefits advice, freelance skills, eLearning, HR admin, job adverts, health and lifecover, and pension plans.

Sales Success links to Winning Business Magazine, and sites specialising in public relations, trade shows, direct marketing, market research, marketing plans and marketing ideas.

Money Matters contains links to the Royal Bank of Scotland's newsletter, business finance from Pintos, insurance from Tolson Messenger (see p.70) and Venturedome for venture capital resources.

Talk and Travel is for planes, trains and automobiles, budget hotels, mobile phones and telecommunications.

IT and the Internet Click here for PC products, computer support, ADSL service, Internet services, domain names and webtop solutions.

Property and Law has a local lawyer search (by postcode) as well as online lawyer links, legal documents, legal assurance, services offices, surveyors and a property search.

Business Supplies covers online auctions (via a link to ebay.co.uk) and online trading, as well as a supplier sourcing search, print and design, and energy supplies.

Help and Advice offers a selection of business books with a direct link to Amazon.co.uk, and a independent review would have been useful. There are practical tips here too: credit reports from Infopromp, a link to David Hall, the business whizz, and insolvency help. The Other Websites page is really helpful with a good chunk of sites under categories for quick reference.

News and Views has links to publications (like Working from Home from homeworking.com – see p.29) and the Federation of Small Businesses (see p.74). There are links to the daily broadsheet papers and a UK briefing search, as well as up-to-the minute business news links.

Smallbiz's strap line is Big Ideas for Small Firms, and though the resources are many and varied, there are not enough links under each topic. How sure can you be that you are seeing the best? Nonetheless a great site for the time poor who want quick answers without trawling a search engine.

www.smallbusinessadvice.org.uk
Small Business Advice

Overall rating: ★ ★ ★ ★ ★			
Classification:	information	**Readability:**	★ ★ ★ ★
Updating:	regular	**Content:**	★ ★ ★ ★ ★
Navigation:	★ ★ ★ ★	**Speed:**	★ ★ ★

UK R

This site, brought to you by the National Federation of Enterprise Agencies, is the one where anyone contemplating launching their own business should start. It welcomes you with the hearty motto 'seize the day' as a free and independent source of advice and information. It is aimed at entrepreneurs, owners managers and the self-employed, or those with a new or established business employing fewer than 10 people, though note it covers England only. The site supplies documents, checklists, business planning software, and links to other useful sites.

SPECIAL FEATURES

Business Advice comes from one of over 200 accredited business advisers who are members of the UK Enterprise agency network and, by postcode, you are linked to your nearest adviser who will have a better understanding of your local business community. Features include a personal communications page in case you don't have email. Enquirers need to register and are allocated a four digit PIN number, and SBA stress that the service is confidential. They claim to be able to deliver a response in 90 per cent of cases within two working days.

Information includes a list of FAQs such as 'What is my best trading status?' 'Funding for business start up' and 'How do I recover outstanding payments?' All this is laid out in a 'real life' question and answer format with sensible and comprehensive answers. Knowledge Base is a rather formal name for an archive of enquiries from which browsers can glean information. It's in its infancy so no advice could be found for a hypothetical enquiry on budgeting for a self-employed person in the communications business.

eBusiness has an excellent outline of what the internet can and, more importantly, cannot do for your business, with questions to ask yourself. Get Email expounds the virtues of having just that with links to Hotmail and Freeserve. Selling on the internet and getting on the web provide advice and have a link to www.the-url.com.

Business Planning offers pointers on getting started and where to go for help and advice, as well as guidelines for existing businesses, business planning and free downloads of Microsoft Word and Excel documents.

Resource Centre has over 45 useful links to sites such as The Confederation of British Industry (see p.100) and the Princes Trust (see p.25), which can be bookmarked; how to find your nearest Local Enterprise Agency (with a click-on-your-area map), and free software which is still under construction.

For Students has a Business Planning page with every detail of the thought processes behind starting a business. This is similar to other pages on the site, but in a more simplified and accessible way.

A really comprehensive site, with sensible advice to give confidence to people dipping in their toe with a new business idea. A great starting point.

www.startups.co.uk
Startups

Overall rating: ★ ★ ★ ★			
Classification:	information	**Readability:**	★ ★ ★ ★
Updating:	regular	**Content:**	★ ★ ★ ★ ★
Navigation:	★ ★ ★ ★	**Speed:**	★ ★ ★

UK

This one really is the business for anyone with an entrepreneurial notion, who wants a resource on all aspects of running a business. It was set up in January 2000 by David Lester, a young whippersnapper with a successful company, Crimson Publishing. Though readers can subscribe via the site to a publication called Start Your Own Business, all the information you will need is free within Startups and the site is supported by pretty top drawer advertisers. Startups modus operandi is to 'inspire entrepreneurs to help start and grow successfully' and though it lacks the gung ho enthusiasm of some sites, it certainly makes up for it in quality and detail.

SPECIAL FEATURES

News and press stories relating to small businesses.

Starting Up covers the very basic points of launching off on your own, in a series of articles. They list these as commitment, motivation, emotional resilience and the pros and cons. Links include a directory of accountants, lawyers and business advisers who have paid to appear on the site.

Finance covers leasing, banks, venture capital, grants, business angels, finance management, factoring and discounting and tax issues relating to small businesses. There is a directory here too under each heading of specialists, and contacts in these areas. The articles are thorough with quotes from experts from, for example, the

British Venture Capital Association (see p.44).

Franchising with the benefits and downsides, case studies and franchise links.

Technology features, supporting the advantages of PCs, networks and the Internet in business – which, given the medium, may well be preaching to the converted.

Equipment Buyer describes and, crucially, reviews business equipment including printers, faxes, scanners and accounting software.

Premises looks at how one should go about finding premises, and provides links to estate agents, serviced offices and regional development authorities.

Working @ home has well-worked features on not only the tax issues and practicalities of working from home, but the emotional issues too, such as loneliness and motivation.

Employment has comprehensive articles covering employing staff, recruitment, staff benefits and pensions, and tax law, with a directory of HR consultants.

Marketing takes the view that there is no point in doing anything unless you tell people about it, and covers fully areas such as direct marketing, advertising, public relations, and marketing online, with asociated directories covering many of the areas.

OTHER FEATURES

Include the Start Up Round Table, a chat forum, feedback on the site, how to advertise and a subscription facility to Crimson Publishing titles. About Us waxes lyrical about Start Ups and is a good example of a business plan in itself.

A thorough, if perhaps overlong, information site which will be invaluable to aspiring entrepreneurs who want a thorough sounding in the ins and outs of starting a business.

www.virginbiz.net
Virgin Business

Overall rating: ★ ★ ★ ★			
Classification:	information	**Readability:**	★ ★ ★ ★
Updating:	regular	**Content:**	★ ★ ★ ★ ★
Navigation:	★ ★ ★ ★	**Speed:**	★ ★ ★

UK

Well, Virgin has to be here somewhere, doesn't it? But curiously there is no mention on the site of Mr Branson and no hints to the secrets of his success. This an information site, with the emphasis on Internet business; the Sitebuilder channel offering advice on building a website and marketing over the web. You get the straight talking we have come to expect from Virgin, and much of it is quite refreshing, but it lets itself down with out-of-date information, the banking section being especially pitiful.

Avoid the busy homepage, where links pop up in a card file style, and head straight for the site map. Here the goodies on offer are laid out in a much simpler and more readable manner. The channels cover managing your business, the business lifecycle (including start-ups), work style (including managing people and working from home), and entrepreneurs (with a rather dubious Tracey's Diary about a freelancer in the women in business section).

SPECIAL FEATURES

Chat Community covers sales, law, IT and small business.

Biz News is updated hourly, with an immediacy that sits strangely with the rest of the site.

Business Advice features are provided by bodies such as Which? and The People Development Partnership.

Toolbox is a good feature with services you can receive back from suppliers and the opportunity to put forward your services.

Bizguide is a step-by-step guide through the important elements of setting up a business, with free Parkes Business Focus software to download. The information (from Parkes) is thorough and helpful.

OTHER FEATURES

New Businesses can be bought off the shelf through the site.

Free Website Trial offers just that and the opportunity to buy personalised documents online.

Online Business Club is run in conjunction with Business Clubs UK, which gives members the chance to meet and make deals with buyers and suppliers from across the country and anticipate and plan for changes in your industry sector by keeping in close contact with others.

Mailing lists can be bought online.

A bit of a curate's egg of a site, with some excellent elements (notably the Bizguide and Toolbox), but in need of some updating in places. There is no facility to return to the home page on many pages and no channel directory within each page. Worth digging for the good stuff, but a definite 'could do better'.

young entrepeneurs sites

www.princes-trust.org.uk				
The Princes Trust				
Overall rating: ★ ★ ★ ★				
Classification:	support		Readability:	★ ★ ★ ★ ★
Updating:	regular		Content:	★ ★ ★ ★ ★
Navigation:	★ ★ ★ ★		Speed:	★ ★ ★ ★ ★
UK				

The Princes Trust has been helping young people, aged 14-30, to 'develop confidence, learn new skills and get into work' for more than 25 years. This colourful, picture-packed site beautifully reflects the get up and go attitude of the Trust, which crows confidently about the 400,000 people it has helped so far. Though the site covers a multitude of subjects relating to young people (rehabilitation of offenders, the homeless, children leaving care, amongst others), it also gives over a healthy chunk to its Business Start Up support. No advice is given directly, just a positive message throughout that you can work for yourself and the links for support and grants (up to £5,000 interest free) are there.

SPECIAL FEATURES

Get Involved gives a list of areas in which the Princes Trust is involved. This includes Work for Yourself, with an email link for those who want to receive Princes Trust Information about Business Start Up support, a Free Call Back service, and a Send a Be Your Own Boss Brochure request link.

What's New gives up to date information about the Prince of Wales's activities in the Trust and Trust events, a list of celebrities supporting the Trust (with tantalising promises that you might be lucky enough to meet the likes of Pierce Brosnan), and features about the Trust. Browsers can access press releases and any research documents carried out by or on behalf of the Trust.

Exchange Ideas includes testimonials from those who have benefited from the Trust (though there are surprisingly few considering the length of time it has been established), and list of partners including BT, Camelot and the Millennium Commission, and links to www.princestrustshop.co.uk (to buy goods made by PT supported enterprises), the DfEE and the National Grid for Learning.

OTHER FEATURES

Other features include a facility to donate to the Trust's work, and keyword search and a very good map of the nearest Princes Trust to you. Click on the map and then the relevant coloured button for the programme that is of interest.

This site is great starting point for young people who want to branch out on their own and who may be eligible for Trust support. Very positive and confident, clearly written with no scary business jargon.

www.shell-livewire.org
Shell Livewire

Overall rating: ★ ★ ★

Classification:	support	Readability:	★★★★★
Updating:	regular	Content:	★★★★★
Navigation:	★★★	Speed:	★★★★★

UK

Another support organisation for young people (18 to 30) who want to start up and develop their own business. Shell Livewire (yes, Shell as in Petrol) was set up in 1982 and also hosts a national competition for business start ups. Not a site to look at first thing in the morning; the home page is bright and flashy, and it's not that easy to sort out where to browse first. However the information is there, set out in simple terms, with plenty of links to further sites.

SPECIAL FEATURES

Information covers a breakdown of the skills young entrepreneurs will need (manager, salesperson, worker, admin) which are a little too brief, and includes a link to a Shell Livewire specialist adviser; The Right Idea has a list of questions to ask yourself before you start (with a link to request a free Business Kit); Test Yourself is a multiple choice quiz to find out what sort of person you are ; FAQs include 'who are my potential customers?' and 'why should I keep financial records?' with very brief answers.

Top Ten Ideas are those received by Shell Livewire (including business plans for a clothes shop, café and graphic design), and here there is more detailed information on setting up these type of businesses, with pros and cons, legal issues, promotion and training, plus further reading and a list of useful addresses.

E-Commerce is covered thoroughly with Q&As as well as links to sites like Web Monkey, eCommerce News and www.isi.gov.uk. There are book recommendations and a link to the sites discussion forum, Business Bites.

What's Happening is a run down of press releases about national Shell Livewire business winners, and Let's Go is a 1.4mb download of quizzes and top ten tips.

The Competition is an important part of the site (currently offering £10,000) for the best business plan. A free Adobe Acrobat download gives you access to business plan outlines and links to local Livewire co-ordinators.

OTHER FEATURES

There's a Lo-Call facility, and a link to www.thebigtrip.co.uk (Shell Livewire's rather curious site for young people unsure about their future, with career planning and help with assessing what they have to offer and registration for a free Business Kit).

An appealing site for young people bubbling with business ideas, but unsure where to go next. A little thin in places but with the right idea.

www.young-enterprise.org.uk
Young Enterprise

Overall rating: ★ ★ ★			
Classification:	information	Readability:	★ ★ ★
Updating:	occasionally	Content:	★ ★ ★ ★ ★
Navigation:	★ ★ ★ ★	Speed:	★ ★ ★ ★
UK			

Founded in 1963, Young Enterprise is a national education charity to inspire and equip young people to learn through enterprise. Its programmes include running a real company, Team Enterprise and Graduate Enterprise. The programme works on a local basis, with volunteers from local businesses coming into schools to advise 14 to 19 year olds on the basics of running a business. Though this is not strictly an essential business site, it is useful for teachers and young people wanting to find out more about the programme, and for entrepreneurs wanting to know how to get involved.

SPECIAL FEATURES

The site shows you how to become involved in and support with the Company Programme: financially, in-kind, and through the provision and encouragement of volunteers. There are also links to regional and national office.

News feature covers events within the Young Enterprise network.

Young Enterprise is a great scheme for businesses wanting to get involved in the community and nurture young talent. A useful information site about YE, but nothing more.

homeworking

www.homebusiness.org.uk
Home Business Alliance

Overall rating: ★ ★ ★ ★			
Classification: information		**Readability:**	★ ★ ★ ★
Updating: monthly		**Content:**	★ ★ ★ ★
Navigation: ★ ★ ★ ★		**Speed:**	★ ★ ★

UK £

According to the Home Business Alliance, six million small enterprises have less than nine employees, and the Alliance's appeal is to that lonely little group (especially the two and a half million who have no employees at all). Though the HBA is a membership organisation, which promotes home working and lobbies decision-making bodies, the advantages of membership don't seem to be huge. The bulk of the HBA information is available free to browsers on the site. The tone is friendly and supportive, they say 'we know what it's like to be self-employed working from home, and we're here for you', and the information is comprehensive and well-targeted.

Broadly, the HBA can offer privileged access to two publications (The Boss and The Board), discounts on services to members, access to a network of business advisers including ex-bank managers (so that's where they go), and the facility to promote your particular skills to businesses looking for home workers. HBA members can add the organisation's logo to their business literature. For those too mean to join, there is plenty of information on effective home working free to air.

SPECIAL FEATURES

Legal queries are answered free by www.lawgym.com (see p.58), and published first in The Boss, then posted on the site. So even if you cannot asked a question without your HBA ID number, you can read the replies. There are no guarantees that your questions will automatically be answered.

The Board is the second subscription publication, looking at the pros and cons of certain businesses (10 each month), with advice on home working scams. Without advertising, it claims to be entirely unbiased.

Lifestyles covers two case studies per month (running a UK business from France for example), and is a thinly veiled advertising vehicle for the businesses themselves, though the content and experiences are useful for reference.

Readers can link to Smarterwork.com, a web design and marketing service, which can also provide PR help and a research facility. There's also a link too to www.e-lancers-world.co.uk, a rather gung-ho site offering free resource pages for home workers – your cyber personal assistant.

Working from Home is a useful feature which could do with appearing higher up the pecking order on the site, and looks at types of home working (such as teleworking and freelancing), and the pros and cons . It also explains types of advisors and gives a list of useful addresses.

Statistics show the DTI's research on businesses with figures on the number of self-employed, and a link to the site.

The Tax Page is a practical guide to taxation which will be most relevant to start-ups, and a useful reference for the maze which is self-employment and business taxation. There's nothing here that can't be found elsewhere, but nicely written and a good one stop guide. Finance is a similar idea, written as a monthly newsletter, by an independent financial adviser.

The Links page lists 21 useful web sites for B2B, including www.homeworking.com and businesseurope.com.

OTHER FEATURES

HBA members can also have privileged access to Credit Union, the organisation's independent financial, savings and loan co-operative. A monthly standing order entitles you to borrow twice your savings after six months, at 1% interest per month.

HBA specialises and cares for a specific group and the information is geared to the home worker and self-employed wanting support and advice. A good resource vehicle.

www.homeworking.com			
Homeworking			
Overall rating: ★ ★ ★ ★			
Classification: information		**Readability:**	★★★★
Updating: regularly		**Content:**	★★★★
Navigation: ★★★★		**Speed:**	★★★
UK			

This site has the edge on The Home Business Alliance in that it is entirely free, and covers as much, if not more, information. Homeworking was set up in early 1999 by a woman who found a dearth of information on the Internet. If anything the emphasis is on women, but as the majority of home workers are often mothers juggling work and parenting, it's a understandable bias. Minor niggles include the slow access speed to certain pages (in fact some were abandoned), and the plethora of exclamation marks, which add nothing to an already upbeat tone.

The homepage features the major aspects of the site, and highlights newsy features for quick reference. Here you will find links to sites such as ebedo and legalshop.co.uk. There's a sell-your-house online facility, and useful link to the Health and Safety Executive for employment and homeworking guidelines. Go to the Main Index though for a clear map of the site, which is split broadly into Personal, Work and Practicalities, with a meaty index under each heading.

SPECIAL FEATURES

Free homeworking.com banner facility for use on your own website.

Personal contains articles on a wide number of issues, with highlights including a link to online psychometric tests (so you can find out what sort of home career suits you, if any!), advice on redundancy and an excellent feature on debt advice, split into categories. The links to other sites have brief reviews and include search engines and sites for women. The case studies number over 40, split broadly into teleworkers, network marketing, freelance, mail order, self-employed and part time.

Work has sound advice on why businesses fail, good start up advice, and majors on scams, the bane of the homeworker. There is information on how to spot scams (with examples of bogus offers) and good links on pyramid selling and the Advertising Standards Authority.

Practicalities covers work space issues, planning permission, using and working on the Internet, and a useful piece on home insurance. More spurious is advice on answering the phone, and Easy Lunchtime (recipes for homeworkers to stop you surviving on the contents of the biscuit tin).

OTHER FEATURES

Readers can give email details for the site's newsletter, and there is a lively feedback forum and soap box, where people can post letters about aspects that irritate them about home working. The books page is excellent, with reviews of several publications on home working issues and a link to amazon.co.uk.

It lifts the spirits to find a site which is well thought out and easy to navigate. Homeworking.com investigates the gentler world outside the rat race (which is why most people plump for it after all). The tone is distinctly feminine. One to bookmark.

OTHER SITES OF INTEREST

Entrepreneur
www.entrepreneur.com
An all-singing, all-dancing US site, with plenty of gung ho language, but if you ignore the US-specific information, there is a raft of useful stuff including start-up advice, writing a business plan, book-keeping basics, marketing, e-business, funding, invoicing and debt collection, computer equipment and software.

Self-Employment
www.selfemployment.co.uk
An excellent online Resource Centre put together in association with Business Development Counsellor/Trainers from across the country who work through Enterprise Agencies. The site covers business planning and support, business information including regulations and marketing strategies, a pre-business checklist (tax, insurance, health and safety), and means for funding finance from grants to venture capital and loans. Well laid out and easy to follow.

Chapter 02

funding & finance

Money, or lack of it, is at the core of most business failures. Funding may not be adequate for suitable marketing, cashflow can mean suppliers are not paid on time, and burgeoning business ideas can be strangled at birth by lack of finance.

Financial issues are dealt with well on the internet, with plenty of sites around to offer advice, financial options (franchising is especially well dealt with) or even make offers of funding. Venture capitalists and private investors especially have a good presence here, and business 'matchmakers' linking investors with enterprises provide a brilliant shortcut to funding the next stage of your expansion. It goes without saying that you should proceed with caution until you are satisfied that offers of financial support are everything they claim to be.

The banks have realised the attraction for customers of being able to access their account information online. For some of the banks this service is in its infancy, but over the next 12 months they will all, no doubt, be providing internet banking facilities for individual and business customers, so we will be able to pay suppliers and move cash around from our desks. The only thing you won't be able to do is pay in your day's takings down the PC. For that, you will still need to pay a visit to your local branch, but who knows what the future holds?

information

www.bankexperts.co.uk
Banking Liaison Group

Overall rating: ★ ★ ★ ★			
Classification:	information	**Readability:**	★ ★ ★ ★
Updating:	occasionally	**Content:**	★ ★ ★ ★
Navigation:	★ ★ ★	**Speed:**	★ ★

UK

So this is where bank managers go when their branches are automated. Run by 'former senior bank managers', and set up in 1991, BLG's aim is to offer business finance and banking advice, and to cut your costs. There is something pin-striped and bowler-hatted about the site, and it must have the least frills of any on the web. But there is something very credible and informed about the information here, and in most cases businesses need to make contact with advisers to pursue their problems further.

SPECIAL FEATURES

Business Banking Check is a free assessment on how your banking arrangements suit your business.

The BLG can check any overcharge on your borrowing (free if the borrowing is over £25,000), and will handle the recovery of your money.

For a fee you can seek assistance in the pursuit of banking disputes.

A bit like having a bank manager on your side for once.

www.obo.org.uk
Banking Ombudsman Scheme

Overall rating: ★ ★ ★ ★ ★			
Classification:	complaints	**Readability:**	★ ★ ★ ★
Updating:	occasionally	**Content:**	★ ★ ★ ★ ★
Navigation:	★ ★ ★ ★	**Speed:**	★ ★ ★ ★

UK

A no-nonsense site which lays out in the clearest terms, when and how you can use the Ombudsman Service to complain about mistreatment from your bank. The service is free and has the power to award up to £100,000.

The instructions are simple and unambiguous, outlining how the Office works, how complaints are dealt with and how you must have reached deadlock (the actual term used by your bank) over a complaint before you can turn to the BOS. There is the facility to complete the complaint form online.

The sort of site you hope you never have to use, but worth knowing about.

http://www.users.globalnet.co.uk/~sblack01/
Black and Williams Management Ltd UK

Overall rating: ★ ★ ★ ★ ★			
Classification:	complaints	Readability:	★ ★ ★ ★
Updating:	occasionally	Content:	★ ★ ★ ★ ★
Navigation:	★ ★ ★ ★	Speed:	★ ★ ★ ★

UK

This is one of those private sites which makes the freedom of speech on the internet worthwhile. It is constructed by Stephen Black, a retired venture capitalist, who describes himself as a 'gamekeeper turned poacher', in other words, an entrepreneur backed by venture capital. Not gospel by any means, but gives sound and often funny advice about how to approach venture capitalists, 'You [the company] are a potential source of joy. All you really have to do is demonstrate that you will not cause pain later'. This is refreshing in a sector which is not known for its hilarity.

The site cuts to the core for those looking for funding, but nervous about how to make the first move and about making the right impression. Rather quaint in its simplicity, the index simply lists the VC process: who to approach, how to approach them, the business plan, the intermediaries, VC's decision criteria, and a tell-it-like-it-is list of companies that are turn-offs to VCs. There are links too to BVCA and the Venture Capital Report (see p.44).

Black is also interested in making private investments in 'interesting areas'.

A great place to find no nonsense advice, with an invitation to fax him questions concerning VC funding. No email details given, because 'I'm fed up with junk mail'. Amen to that.

www.bba.org.uk
British Bankers Association

Overall rating: ★ ★ ★			
Classification:	information	Readability:	★ ★ ★
Updating:	regularly	Content:	★ ★ ★ ★
Navigation:	★ ★ ★	Speed:	★ ★ ★

UK

Not the most dynamic site, but a good starting point if you are looking for a business bank account. This is the central information resource for banking information and developments generally.

SPECIAL FEATURES

Small Business Advice gives a brief checklist to consider when setting up, but has plenty of sound information on opening a bank account and raising finance. It covers stakeholder pensions, with a link to the DSS site, trading internationally (with a link to the Euro section of the Dti site) and adopting better payment practice.

Complaints procedures are outlined for when you have an axe to grind with your bank, and there is general advice on reducing bank charges and tax saving tips, with links to Debtline and the Citizens Advice Bureau.

Business Account Finder is an excellent resource for comparing latest accounts, charges, interest and borrowing rates.

One to keep referring to every now and then, especially if you need to complain about your bank.

www.moneytimes.co.uk		
MoneyTimes		
Overall rating: ★ ★ ★ ★		
Classification: portal	Readability:	★ ★ ★ ★
Updating: daily	Content:	★ ★ ★ ★
Navigation: ★ ★ ★ ★ ★	Speed:	★ ★ ★ ★
UK		

Look no further if you want to find a list and links to all the UK's banks, including business account holders and online banking. This is the main directory of all the UK's financial services providers, with thousands of links. Even if you're not looking, go to it just to have fun playing with the letters on the homepage which dance around after your mouse icon.

SPECIAL FEATURES

Business Services for Banks is an introduction for business customers.

Banking and Savings is a directory that allows you to source online banks.

Great reference site, especially for those looking for the right bank for their business.

banks

These sites are usually free to air, but you need to login to use the internet banking facility.

www.abbeynational.co.uk		
Abbey National Group		
Overall rating: ★ ★ ★ ★ ★		
Classification: bank	Readability:	★ ★ ★ ★
Updating: regularly	Content:	★ ★ ★ ★ ★
Navigation: ★ ★ ★ ★ ★	Speed:	★ ★ ★ ★
UK		

A chunky appealing site, which doesn't complicate the banking issue. The information is about accounts and services only, with no business advice available on the site. This can be obtained via the Call Me service. Business Banking services are not immediately obvious. You need to go to Accounts and Services in the index, then to Business Banking. To navigate the site, use the colour-coded boxes at the bottom of the page, with the subject appearing when the mouse icon is placed on them. A nice touch which removes the excess of wording common to many other sites, but the lack of a homepage link is annoying.

Abbey National is aiming at the small business person in terms of employees, not turnover. It's big selling point at the moment is indefinite free banking for sole traders and two person partnerships, who keep their Business Bank Account in credit and raise no more than 25 cheques per month.

SPECIAL FEATURES
As well as the free banking facility, Abbey National offers online, phone, ATM and postal banking to businesses 24/7.

Business Bank Account holders can deposit and request withdrawals, obtain balance advice and account information, additional statements and pay bills this way. The site has a facility to print out an application form and to download Adobe Acrobat.

Business Reserve Account pays interest on accounts with funds up to £2 million, allowing five withdrawals per month or unlimited charged withdrawals by CHAPS. This facility would appeal to sole traders, partnerships, limited companies and charities. Current Interest Rates in the drop down menu outlines interest from 0.40 per cent net per annum to 3.8 per cent net for accounts of £500,000 or over.

Time Deposit Account is Abbey National's fixed rate, fixed term account. For this you need a minimum deposit of £20,000, and fixed rates from 28 days up to one year at four day's notice. Interest is paid gross annually.

OTHER FEATURES

The site incorporates information about personal banking too, as well as information about Stakeholder Pensions and insurance which is relevant to small business people.

Refreshing in its simplicity, Abbey National is not trying to keep up with the big boys. The information is easy to access and explained with the understanding that your banking arrangements are not the be all and end all of your business activities. Would suit sole traders/small partnerships with simple banking transactions.

www.smallbusiness.barclays.co.uk
Barclays Bank Business Banking

Overall rating: ★ ★ ★ ★			
Classification:	bank	**Readability:**	★ ★ ★ ★
Updating:	regularly	**Content:**	★ ★ ★ ★ ★
Navigation:	★ ★ ★ ★	**Speed:**	★ ★ ★ ★

UK

Barclays has always been a slick operator (it was the first to offer customers internet banking), and this site is no exception. It gives details of the resources the bank has to offer small businesses, as well as the facility to apply for an internet account online. The bank has grasped the potential of the web in a big way, and has a step-by-step internet banking demonstration, leaving some competitors behind.

SPECIAL FEATURES

Internet Business Banking allows customers to transfer funds, pay bills and amend standing orders and direct debits. There is free internet access through Business Barclays.net.

Free Banking until 2003 for new customers and 20 per cent saving on bank charges for existing customers. Business and personal account details can be shown together.

Advice is extensive and covers start-ups, established business help, future plans, products and services (including seminars and events), online solutions (including registering a domain name, computer leasing, and setting up an internet business). There is a link too to the Woolwich and Clearly Business (see p.17).

Barclays is a powerful operator in the banking sector and this site reflects that. Full to the brim with good stuff.

www.natwest.com
Natwest

Overall rating: ★ ★ ★ ★ ★			
Classification: bank		**Readability:**	★ ★ ★ ★
Updating: regularly		**Content:**	★ ★ ★ ★ ★
Navigation: ★ ★ ★ ★		**Speed:**	★ ★ ★ ★
UK			

NatWest claims the high ground of being the number one banking choice of small business owners for over 11 years. It's a labyrinthine site, with boxes leading to boxes (there's a search facility, though no site map). You will need to be light of touch as the links are rather flimsy and sensitive. But for all that, the information is very much there. Split broadly into three section, the Small Business sector covers Accounts and Services, Services for Your Sector and Tips and Guidance. Some information is repeated within these sections, but that helps to make sure you miss nothing.

SPECIAL FEATURES

Bank Line Cash Manager Four online banking options from the basic model to a deluxe version.

Agricultural Business has its own special support system including mortgages, farm loans and explains the role of Agricultural Business managers.

Professional Support is for practices, from barristers to chiropodists, and a banking facility for legal eagles (this is called, somewhat confusingly Legal Centre, but is not a legal advice line).

Business Finance for expanding businesses comes from Lombard and there is an email link for further information.

Start-up Help is in abundance, with practical advice from BOSS, the Business One Stop Shop, as well as facilities

including free independent advice, free software and guides, and free banking.

An excellent resource for small businesses and a great advert for the services the bank has to offer. Competitors may cover the logistics of small business better, but Nat West has some interesting specialist services. Don't be heavy handed with the mouse when clicking on links.

www.alliancebusinessbanking.co.uk
Alliance Leicester Business Banking

Overall rating: ★ ★ ★ ★			
Classification:	bank	Readability:	★ ★ ★ ★
Updating:	occasionally	Content:	★ ★ ★ ★
Navigation:	★ ★ ★ ★	Speed:	★ ★ ★ ★

UK

Alliance Leicester has joined with Girobank, so this site covers both banks with a Post Office depositing facility. This site will appeal to small businesses who don't want to bank with of one of the big four. The emphasis right from the homepage is on good service and 'business banking made easy', with a £10 per month flat fee banking package. The index is simple and clear, and the pages short and to the point. It lacks business advice, and focuses more on services it can offer.

SPECIAL FEATURES

Account Manager Internet and PC banking are here, though the PC banking is for corporations with a turnover of more than £1 million. Subscribers need to have an Alliance account to use the internet service. There is a unique free banking facility for Clubs and Societies, and other non-profit making organisations, so long as they stay in credit.

OTHER FEATURES

Links take you to Net Shopping Solutions, www.yourlocalprinter.com, Sovereign Asset Finance and Sovereign Fleet and Spot a Bargain.

As a bank, it may not offer enough for your business. As a site it is clear and easy to follow, with no jargon and a refreshing message.

www.bankofscotland.co.uk/business
Bank of Scotland

Overall rating: ★ ★ ★ ★			
Classification:	bank	Readability:	★ ★ ★ ★
Updating:	occasionally	Content:	★ ★ ★ ★ ★
Navigation:	★ ★ ★ ★	Speed:	★ ★ ★

UK

A clearly laid out site that advertises the products of the bank, and gives login access to the Internet banking facility. Highlights are listed down the centre panel, with a Product of the Month (insurance for example), Direct Business Banking (by phone, freepost and free internet service), Asset financing and vehicle management. There's a facility to download PDF files, and a comprehensive index of services. Icons at the bottom of the page take you to other areas of the Bank (personal banking, students, homebuying and so on).

Like its competitors, Bank of Scotland specialises in businesses services with a resource centre for business learning online or through CDRom.

SPECIAL FEATURES

Useful Websites is not really, with a pretty thin selection of sites, but there is an Internet Banking Tour. Things may change after the proposed merger with Halifax however.

Business Resources has good European business coverage with guides, documents and FAQs, including a free DTI CDRom about the Euro.

The Business Travel and Accommodation facility includes online booking, specially negotiated rates, consolidated fares and management reports normally available to larger companies. There are Bonus Travelpoints too.

BoS Internet powered by BT Click, provides direct access to the Internet and the bank's website, and there is a full time internet helpdesk (in case you feel the urge to call on Christmas Day).

As with the other banks, Bank of Scotland wants your business but is not so bold as to ask for it. Good information, generally speaking, but nothing much to grab you and make you say 'Yes, I must put my business here'.

www.banking.hsbc.co.uk/business
HSBC Business Banking

Overall rating: ★★★★			
Classification:	bank	Readability:	★★★★
Updating:	occasionally	Content:	★★★★★
Navigation:	★★★★	Speed:	★★★

UK

The HSBC site is just an advertisement for the services of the big high street bank. It stresses the supportive role the bank will have in your business, with business advisers in each branch, but is pretty thin on actual hard facts. You will need to visit a branch.

SPECIAL FEATURES

Starting a Business section has plenty of facts and a free helpline for the first year of trading, plus a couple of audio files on holiday entitlements and P45s. There are discounts too on Pegasus Capital Lite software, and a business pack with details of two year's free banking.

HSBC's unique sales pitch is that it has not raised its small business tariff for 10 years.

The Finance Raising section provides information on the various ways to raise capital. Clear and well-explained.

www.success4business.com
Lloyds TSB

Overall rating: ★ ★ ★			
Classification:	bank	Readability:	★ ★ ★ ★
Updating:	regularly	Content:	★ ★ ★ ★ ★
Navigation:	★ ★ ★	Speed:	★ ★

UK R

Visit this site for business banking information, as the bank's main site is for personal customers only (though there are links on it to MarketPlace Solutions, Asset Finance and Commercial, which is for businesses with an annual turnover of £2 million plus).

Lloyds TSB Businesses customers have access to telephone banking, internet banking, TV banking and the facility to deposit cheques at the Post Office.

Lloyds TSB offers more even than Barclays, but much is registration only. The idea is that you don't waste time browsing for information that isn't relevant to you. By clicking on the picture/area which applies to your business (Starting Out, Going for Growth – which has a rather appropriate picture of a man in dire need of a shave – Making It Easier, New Directions and Just Looking) and registering, each time you login you will be taken immediately to the area you want. These advantages are not entirely convincing (you have to register again for Essential Business Advice), and the pages are very slow to load.

SPECIAL FEATURES

Business Directory is available once you've registered on the site,and allows you to add your own business details to the list. It offers tailored business services, solutions advice, special offers, a communication forum and news (you can choose from a list of news areas).

Links include the Met Office, RAC, Inland Revenue, Customs and Excise amongst others.

www.royalbankofscotland.co.uk/small_business			
Royal Bank of Scotland			
Overall rating: ★ ★ ★ ★			
Classification:	bank	**Readability:**	★ ★ ★ ★
Updating:	regularly	**Content:**	★ ★ ★ ★ ★
Navigation:	★ ★ ★	**Speed:**	★ ★
UK			

The superior of the two Scottish banks' sites, with a heavy sales pitch, but with very few of its goods on show in the shop window. The site expounds the virtues of its branch based Relationship Managers, and is surprisingly less boastful of its online services. To find internet banking details takes some sleuthing: go to Business Banking Direct, Managing Your Day to Day Banking, Current Accounts, and finally Online Banking. Alternatively you could do a site search. The whole site is a warren for information, and the best search option is the A to Z of services.

SPECIAL FEATURES

A business plan software CD and PC discount offer with Gateway PC suppliers.

Starting Your Business lists good information on financing options available, including development loans, and access to The Royal Bank's quarterly newsletter, Royal Business, dedicated to new and existing small businesses.

The Bank's Mentor Facility is designed to help keep businesses up-to-date with employment and health and safety law.

Hidden in the site are some gems of information and business support, but considering the competition they are up against, browsers would be forgiven for giving up and going elsewhere. Worth sticking with if you have the time.

www.ybonline.co.uk			
Yorkshire Bank			
Overall rating: ★ ★ ★ ★			
Classification:	bank	**Readability:**	★ ★ ★ ★
Updating:	regularly	**Content:**	★ ★ ★ ★
Navigation:	★ ★ ★	**Speed:**	★ ★ ★
UK			

Though not one of the big boys, Yorkshire Bank is a significant presence in the banking line up, and is a popular business bank. Its foreign credentials are impressive (it's a wholly owned subsidiary of National Australia Group Limited) and has links with Clydesdale Bank PLC based in Glasgow, Northern Bank Limited based in Belfast and National Irish Bank Limited based in Dublin. The simplicity of the website will appeal to those not wanting to be bombarded with lists and links. Simple boxes take you to business banking, online share dealing as well as personal banking and news. Site does have a few link hiccups however.

SPECIAL FEATURES

Same day **CHAPS** transfer facility.

Yorpay, a rather ugly word for a payment facility for up to 250 employees or suppliers at the same time.

Financing Options (including vehicle contract hire) and Business Term Deposits, short term high rate investment opportunities.

Farm Services including access to an Agribusiness Manager.

Not in the same league as some of the High Street banks, but worth a look if your business demands are not too complicated. Some links are sleepy.

Other sites with business banking:

Bank of Ireland
www.bankofireland.co.uk/business_banking

Norwich and Peterborough Building Society
www.npbs.co.uk

Standard Chartered
www.standardchartered.com

Barclays Business Park
www.businesspark.barclays.com
An excellent site for business, including statistics (in the section marked Bulletin) on business trends, and shopping facility for computers and telecoms.

raising funding

www.british-franchising.org			
British Franchising Association			
Overall rating: ★ ★ ★ ★			
Classification:	information	**Readability:**	★ ★ ★ ★ ★
Updating:	occasionally	**Content:**	★ ★ ★ ★ ★
Navigation:	★ ★ ★ ★ ★	**Speed:**	★ ★ ★ ★ ★
UK			

If you are thinking of becoming a franchisee, or of franchising out your business, this is the place to look first. Top marks all round for this site, which realises all the potential of the web with concise readable information in an easy to navigate site, and plenty of intelligent comment.

Franchise, by which a license is granted to others to sell an existingproduct or service, is a thriving concern (think of The Body Shop, Clarks Shoes, Prontaprint ...), and the BFA are keen to point out (often!) that 96% of franchises are still in profit after five years, compared to 45% of small businesses. The BFA's aim in to put potential franchisees in touch with franchisers, to advise people dipping their toe in, in whichever role, and to help franchisers to follow the BFA code of ethical conduct.

The opening page has links to site sponsors Barclays, HSBC, Lloyds TSB, NatWest and the Royal Bank of Scotland, and a quick link takes you to the BFA homepage. The screen in split into three columns almost throughout, with the question or subject in the left column, and answer in the centre column. On the homepage, the third column is used for listing diary dates of International franchising exhibitions, press releases and the chance to subscribe to the BFA's newsletter, Newsline.

SPECIAL FEATURES

The extensive package of information includes advice about choosing the right franchise. The case studies are good (with not all the companies included being the big hitters), and there is an email link to www.whichfranchise.org where you can order a BFA-endorsed CD rom and Video.

BFA Directory of accredited members and advisers, with addresses and links to their websites.

European Franchise Federation and the **World Franchise Council** lists details on foreign franchises.

Costing Out a Franchise The site clearly explains how the franchiser receives an initial fee from the franchisee, payable at the outset, together with on-going management service fees - usually based on a percentage of annual turnover or mark-ups on supplies. In return, the franchisor has an obligation to support the franchise network, notably with training, product development, advertising, promotional activities and with a specialist range of management services.

The BFA clearly lays out the benefits to the franchisor of membership, including:
- Recognition as one of the best franchisors.
- Exclusive access to BFA franchises recruitment systems.
- The best advice and experience through National and Regional meetings.
- Access to accredited professional advisers
- Training and seminar programs specifically designed for franchising.
- Discounts on exhibitions, advertising and other costs.
- Automatic entry to BFA accredited national franchise exhibitions.
- Independent arbitration scheme for alternative dispute resolution.
- Protection from unwarranted legislation in the UK and Europe.

- Exclusive access to the prestigious Franchisor of the Year Awards sponsored by the Midland Bank and the Daily Express.

And benefits to the franchisee of BFA Membership:
- Identification of franchisors willing and able to meet published standards of good practice.
- Ongoing commitment on the part of franchisors to act ethically and keep up with best practice.
- Access to accredited professional advisors.
- Access to low cost complaints and arbitration schemes should a dispute arise.
- BFA endorsement of your franchise network to make the sale of your business easier.
- Protection from unwarranted legislation in the UK and Europe.
- Access to exhibitions and seminars meeting BFA standards.

If franchising is your interest, this is an excellent resource. Almost all details are online, and it allows you to make an informed choice.

www.whichfranchise.org
Which Franchise

Overall rating: ★ ★ ★			
Classification:	information	**Readability:**	★ ★ ★ ★
Updating:	weekly	**Content:**	★ ★ ★ ★
Navigation:	★ ★ ★ ★	**Speed:**	★ ★ ★

UK

This should be the second stop after www.british-franchising.org, its affiliated site (see p.41). Though there is some information for franchisors (how to put together an Operational Manual or promote their business, for example), the site is really aimed at franchisees, to help them 'evaluate franchise opportunities'.

Set up by franchise expert, Johnny Sellyn, it's a slow site, not helped by three indexes that leave one at a loss as to where to start. Busy, busy, busy, and all the mass of information does is hide some very intelligent and sensible advice from franchise experts, many from the leading high street banks.

The right hand column throughout the site lists specially featured franchises with profiles of each company and links.

The site index along the top of the homepage includes advice on financial issues and legal issues, both written by bankers and solicitors (all BFA affiliated). These lead you by the hand through the franchising system, and if anything is not covered, there is an Ask the Expert forum, with answers emailed back to you.

SPECIAL FEATURES

UK Franchise Search Enter details on the Search under name of franchise, minimum personal investment and industry sector for a short cut to a suitable franchise business.

Which Franchise supplies details on franchise resales, free reports and consultations and details of franchising in Scotland.

Links on the homepage take you to updated features, with a different business area featured each month. There is also news and testimonials from contented franchisees.

OTHER FEATURES

Advice also includes choosing a franchise, with the hints and tips page being no more than a list of quotes from franchisors and experts.

Where Else to Look is a useful redirection point with details of the four annual BFA credited exhibitions, magazines and directories, an interactive CD rom, Cdfex, and information about business start up advisors, Business Link and Small Business Gateway (Scotland), which strangely have no web link, just a phone number.

Noticeboard allows you to register your interest in franchises in specific areas, which includes details such as your experience and the amount you are able to invest.

A very good resource of information and advice, which gets better the further into the site you delve.

www.bvca.co.uk
British Venture Capital Association

Overall rating: ★ ★ ★			
Classification:	information	**Readability:**	★ ★ ★ ★
Updating:	occasionally	**Content:**	★ ★ ★ ★
Navigation:	★ ★ ★ ★	**Speed:**	★ ★ ★ ★

UK

Venture capital is an excellent option for entepreneurs wanting investment of over £10,000. It provides long-term, committed, risk-sharing equity capital, without the loan repayment pressure small businesses would receive from banks. According to the information on the site, the UK industry is the largest and most developed in Europe accounting for 49% of total annual venture capital investment. The UK venture capital industry has spent £29 billion in Britain since 1983.

Though the BVCA does not cover all UK venture capital organisations and private equity, it represents the majority, so the site is a good source for information about how venture capital works, and details of affiliated advisers.

SPECIAL FEATURES

Directory includes a questionnaire about the amount you are looking to raise, in which sector, for what purpose and the geographical location (world-wide). Your details will generate a list of potential investors, though interest is not guaranteed! The Members List has firms by name, which include professional advisers, financial organisations, capital firms, and academic or honorary members. Each listing has a profile of the companies, how much they usually invest (in the case of capital firms), and who to contact.

Sources of Advice covers member solicitors (44 listed), corporate finance and management/business advisers,

financial and management services, accountants and tax advisers. Each listing has the CV of the firm and contacts.

Downloads are free and available from the list of publications and BVCA research, with a free Adobe Acrobat reader download too.

Venture Capital contains information about the nature of venture capital and the work of the BVCA. The information is good, with facts and figures on why venture capital is a good option. There's a list of quoted and unquoted companies, many whose names you will recognise, who have found success with venture capital backing.

Private Equity gives details of entrepreneurs and management teams.

Latest contains press releases, which are updated monthly with an index by subject, but with some sections out of date.

OTHER FEATURES

Other Finance covers financiers, secondary purchasers and gatekeepers for larger organisations, so may not be relevant to small businesses. Nor is the BVCA members' area, which is registration only and contains publications and technical and regulatory bulletins, and a listing of BVCA events.

There is information here too for potential investors, including VDCITs, venture capital trusts and Business Angel Investment.

The site is playing two roles: information for members and a resource for small businesses looking for investment. There is probably not enough information for the latter, who might be better finding more extensive information about venture capital as a financing option (and the potential risks) elsewhere before using the members contact listings.

www.firsttuesday.com
First Tuesday

Overall rating: ★ ★ ★			
Classification: financing		**Readability:**	★★★★
Updating: daily		**Content:**	★★★★
Navigation: ★★★★		**Speed:**	★★★★

UK INT

The odd name for this site comes about because this global meeting place and market place for start-ups had its first event on the first Tuesday in October 1998. On the website (and at First Tuesday events) entrepreneurs can connect with a network of more than 6000 venture capitalists, business angels and private investors from around the world. Since its conception, more than 25 000 people have attended events world-wide each month.

Entrepreneurs looking for backing are invited to submit a business plan via the website, which is then screened and matched to interested investors. You are then invited to a matchmaking event. From the original meeting the set up boasts a global network of over 100,000 subscribers.

SPECIAL FEATURES

FAQs gives the basic information in an easy pop up menu format. Here you'll find information about costs of using the service: it charges a 2 per cent success fee on financing facilitated by its matchmaking events.

First Tuesday Forum is an online discussion group for the European Internet industry,

First Tuesday Jobs helps start-ups find personnel in 24 cities across Europe, via email and the Web. The online job search is via Yahoo.

Daily News Round-up is an emailed newsletter.

First Tuesday Offices is an online exchange of under-utilised office space across Europe, again generated by Yahoo.

Features include writing a successful business plan and how to protect your ideas. The site recommends a rather feeble handful of business books too, with a direct link to Amazon.co.uk.

An interesting idea, which isn't sold too well on the site. Particularly useful for businesses with global ambitions, though First Tuesday's roots are firmly British.

www.nban.co.uk
National Business Angels Network

Overall rating: ★ ★ ★ ★			
Classification:	financing	**Readability:**	★ ★ ★
Updating:	regularly	**Content:**	★ ★ ★ ★
Navigation:	★ ★ ★ ★	**Speed:**	★ ★ ★ ★

UK

National Business Angels Network is a non-profit organisation, sponsored by major financial institutions and the high street banks, and supported by the Department of Trade and Industry. Its role is to source risk capital for small and medium businesses from private investors (or 'business angels') in return for shares in the business.

Business Angels are usually well-off individuals (though they sometimes work in syndicates) with spare capital to put into your company. The average investment is between £25,000 and £1 million, but by their very nature are discreet and elusive people. Estimates suggest however that there are 18,000 Business Angels in the UK actively looking to make investments, investing around £500 million a year in around 3,500 businesses; that's considerably more than venture capital funds. They are angels because they could be the answer to your prayers, and NBAN is a sort of financial dating agency to get the two parties together. The matchmaking is done by NBAN Associates, a nation-wide network of experts (including Business Link and accountants). They are the lynch pin and screen applications via Bestmatch.co.uk, the secure site which interested parties can access and login to through the NBAC site home page once they have registered.

Though the site has a strange order (About Associates comes after the Registration page), there is plenty of information about the NBAN set up, who the Associates are,

how much the service costs and the benefits. There are plenty of sobering statistics too for potential investors about the percentage of company failures, though a possible 50 per cent return on your investment might sugar the pill.

SPECIAL FEATURES

Site Map is a good starting point, showing what is available better than the home page. Though to find about business angels as a concept go to resource on the homepage index›facts and figures or FAQs.

Links include all the sponsoring banks and companies, the DTI website and LIFFOE (the London Futures Exchange) and AIM at the Stock Exchange.

Bulletin is a monthly list of investment opportunities sent to investors registered with NBAN, with free advertising in The Daily Telegraph, and a list of local programmes organised by Associates.

BestMatch is the online matchmaking service, available by registration only, which puts investors together with companies looking for investment. Application to become an investor, investee or Associate can be made online. There is a 30 minutes time out security measure.

About Associates offers a local search facility by postcode and speciality, or alphabetically. You can view the details of a particular expert and then select them.

Good information on the Business Angel system. There is some business jargon, but the language becomes more user friendly as the site gets into its stride. Worth looking at if you've an interesting start-up venture, are looking to expand, or have the odd £100,000 you could afford to lose.

www.real-deals.co.uk
Real Deals Magazine

Overall rating: ★ ★ ★

Classification:	magazine	Readability:	★ ★ ★
Updating:	regularly	Content:	★ ★ ★ ★
Navigation:	★ ★ ★	Speed:	★ ★ ★ ★

UK R £

This is the online facility of the private equity and venture capital magazine, Real Deals, published by Caspian Publishing, which is for venture capitalists, but also useful for those on the receiving end of private financing. Some areas of the site are subscriber only, but much of the news and features pages are free-to-air. Use the online subscribe page to order an annual subscription.

SPECIAL FEATURES

The Vulture is the 'Nigel Dempster' page of the publication, full off gossip and who's doing what where.

Advertisers Llinks are useful for those looking for private equity support or legal advice, though of course they do not come with Real Deal's recommendation.

Done Deals (login only) gives a round-up of venture capital and private equity deals in Europe, with details divided by industry sector, key investors and advisers.

Real Data service gives information on specific deals, industry trends, acquisition targets, adviser rankings and overall deal activity. You pay by credit card only for the information you request which is then supplied to you in Excel.

For SMEs looking for venture capital backing, this one is worth referring to for information, and up-to-date news on activities in the VC sector.

www.vcr1978.com
Venture Capital Report

Overall rating: ★ ★ ★ ★

Classification:	financing	Readability:	★ ★ ★
Updating:	sporadically	Content:	★ ★ ★ ★
Navigation:	★ ★ ★	Speed:	★ ★ ★

UK R £

Venture Capital Report is an associate member of the British Venture Capital Association and is the UK's foremost business angel network, matching private investors seeking to raise money with entrepreneurs seeking equity capital.

The site is broadly split between people wanting to invest, and those looking for backing of £150,000 up to £2 million. Entrepreneurs provide a full and detailed business plan to VCR. This should include an executive summary, a description of the business, financial projections, key management CVs, information on the market and competitors, details of the marketing strategy, details of what the funds will be used for, the proposed financial structure and exit strategy.

Once passed the screening process, VCR will write a four to five page comprehensive summary of your business opportunity and publish it both in the VCR monthly Report and online in the subscriber area to 600 individuals. There is also the opportunity to present to investors at a bi-monthly presentations held in central London.

An article in the monthly Report costs £495 + VAT. This provides you with a comprehensive page summary featuring in-depth information on your business plan; including market, competition, management, product/service and cashflow forecasts. Assuming you and the VCR adviser agree to go ahead at your meeting, this fee will be payable at the end of the meeting before the adviser starts writing.

VCR charges entrepreneurs a success fee for five per cent of capital raised (+VAT). VCR also requires share options giving them the right to buy a small percentage of your company's equity on the same terms as our investors. VCR is regulated by the Securities and Futures Authority.

SPECIAL FEATURES

Resource Centre is the meat of the site, with free downloads of sample legal documents. The links to other sites (venture capitalists, advisory services, government, stock exchange et al) are worth noting.

VCR Directory of investment opportunities.

Current Opportunites are only available to registered members, though a taster about interesting companies looking for investment is featured on the home page.

Workshops are held regularly (many run by VCR's founder Lucius Cary) though some of the details are out of date.

OTHER FEATURES

News Headlines include press releases with investment news and the publications link includes the Venture Capital Handbook, and Lucius Cary's Guide to Raising Capital for the Small Business, both available to order online. Books includes recommendations, and a link to the Global Investment Bookshop.

You can download VCR's business plan criteria in Adobe's Acrobat format.

The ability to promote your business and find suitable backing is fundamentally good use of the web. There isn't much 'we're here to help you' feel good factor about it. But it serves its purpose efficiently and with suitable gravitas.

OTHER SITES OF INTEREST

For young people's business support see: The Princes Trust (p.25) and Shell Livewire (p.26).

Black and Williams Venture Capital Guide
http://www.users.globalnet.co.uk/~sblack01/vc2.htm
Good advice for approaching venture capitalists.

The European Venture Capital Association
www.evca.com

Levy Gee
www.levygee.co.uk
The site is an advertisement for the services of accountants and business advisers, Levy Gee, who have offices in several locations. It is a full service company offering business development support, corporate finance, asset based lending, tax planning and more, but has a venture capital database too with links to venture capital companies. It's well put together, with good basic information, though the aim is obviously to have you make contact.

Market Entry Partnership
www.market-entry.co.uk
A simple site consisting of a few pages. You are asked questions as to where you want to take your business, then Solution tells you what MEP can do for you; which is business advice, assistance with objectives, management services, sourcing project finance. Go to Team for pictures and profiles of the MEP team and details of how to contact them.

Price Waterhouse Coopers
www.pricewaterhousecoopers.co.uk
The Manchester United of business advisers, but worth a look for enterprises which are more medium than small. On the site you'll find Private Equity under Services. Access it via the Corporate Finance and United Kingdom sub-sections.

Chapter 03

legal & financial advice

Is there really such a thing as free legal advice? It seems there might be. Law firms have grasped the potential of the internet with both hands and there is now a significant number of excellent legal websites that can answer legal queries quickly, in some cases immediately and for simple queries the answers can be found for free. Most of these sites specify that they contain information, not specific advice, but many have directories of lawyers in your area, and some are categorised by specialism.

If you do choose to use the virtual lawyers, beware that their fees are not higher than meeting one face to face, and ensure that they have Law Society accreditation. It will come as no suprise that these sites all include a raft of terms and conditions, and as with all legal issues on the web, you are advised to read them.

Financial advice on issues such as your obligations as an employer are there too, and though most finance issues vary depending on each circumstance, the directory facility for finding a financial adviser who specialises in your needs is invaluable and time-saving.

Cashflow is the biggest bugbear of any business, whether a small operation or a sole trader. Too many companies go under as a result of bad debts and reliance on orders not yet paid for. Too much time is wasted chasing un-paid invoices, and the plethora of debt collection companies will be a welcome support system.

payment support

www.equifax.co.uk
Equifax

Overall rating: ★ ★ ★			
Classification:	credit info	Readability:	★ ★ ★
Updating:	regularly	Content:	★ ★ ★ ★
Navigation:	★ ★ ★	Speed:	★ ★ ★

UK R £ 🔒

The UK arm of the big US credit-checking company, Equifax has full reports on over 1.5 million UK limited companies and 1.4 million non-limited ones. It can also provide small businesses with credit limit details on limited and non-limited companies for credit insurance purposes. Details can be paid for on subscription or individually.

The site's resources are also invaluable for the self-employed homeworker should they need to check on their personal credit profile. At a cost of £2.50 payable by credit card (the site supports secure payment), you will receive details of credit details held about you. Useful if you need a loan or to re-mortgage to raise capital.

SPECIAL FEATURES

Customer Service Teams are available locally to business subscribers.

Links to profiles on companies world-wide. There are also links to www.ebtob-uk.com, which offers a business to business profile service.

An invaluable service for growing businesses. Worth bookmarking for its business to business service alone.

www.csa-uk.com
The Credit Services Association

Overall rating: ★ ★ ★			
Classification:	credit info	Readability:	★ ★ ★ ★
Updating:	regularly	Content:	★ ★ ★ ★
Navigation:	★ ★ ★ ★	Speed:	★ ★ ★ ★

UK

The Credit Services Association (not to be confused with the other CSA) is the only National Association in the UK for Debt Recovery Agencies and Allied Professional Credit Services. The site is really a directory of members, which are organised under category and alphabetically. Categories include Business to Business and International Debt Collection, Tracing and Company Searches. Find the service you require, go to 'members in alphabetical order' on the site index, and click on the relevant letter in the box on the right. For a complete list, click on 'All'. CSA members are also listed by UK region. For members there are details of the CSA's code of conduct.

The Free document download has features including starting up and employment in a debt collection agency. The information is brief. The newsletter and press releases are out of date, if dated at all.

The site is thin on information, but a useful resource for company listings. There is no complaints facility though, which does undermine the authority of the organisation.

www.payontime.co.uk
The Better Payment Practice Campaign

Overall rating: ★ ★ ★ ★			
Classification:	payment	**Readability:**	★ ★ ★ ★ ★
Updating:	regularly	**Content:**	★ ★ ★ ★ ★
Navigation:	★ ★ ★ ★	**Speed:**	★ ★ ★ ★

UK

The Better Payment Practice Group (BPPG) works as a service to help both suppliers and buyers tackle the late payment issue. The site provides links to small business support groups – The Forum for Private Business, the Small Business Service, British Bankers Association amongst others (see elsewhere for reviews of their sites) – and its main purpose is the publication of a guide to 'improve the payment culture of the UK business community and reduce the incidence of late payment of commercial debt'.

Throughout the site there are grim reminders of the consequences of unpaid invoices and late payment, and the features are all geared to help small businesses keep an eye on cashflow, check references of new customers, and chase up outstanding payments. The site is simple to use, though one gripe is the lack of a quick homepage link, and there is no contact number for the BPPG.

SPECIAL FEATURES

BPPG Guide is 28 pages long, and can be found in the link down the left hand side of the homepage, where is can be downloaded.

Late Payment of Commercial Debts (Interest) Act 1998 is a User's Guide in PDF. Much of the information in the former, written by Credico Ltd, appears as the core of the website anyway, though it includes details of how to apply to use the BPPG logo.

Collect the Cash includes useful templates for invoice chasing and payment term letters, risk reduction techniques, exporting, and how to check credit worthiness, which has links to information about credit agencies, the Companies Act, Register of County Court Judgements, amongst others.

Quick Step questions serves as a sort of site round-up, with a checklist of questions you should ask yourself when taking on a new account.

The Support Group links are good, with web links, addresses phone and fax numbers. Listed organisation include Companies House, Confederation of British Industry, Institute of Credit Management and the British Standards Institute.

Business Doctor is an question and answer facility, with a reply promised within five days. The service carries a hefty disclaimer however.

News had not been updated for two months at time of writing, but there is an email link to the BPPG's PR agency for current new items and press releases. One press release buried back in 1999 featured the top reasons and excuses for late payments. These included such gems as 'I cannot make payment until the planets are aligned, which is only twice a year' and 'We're in the middle of an armed robbery'. If you are browsing the BPPG site it may be because you've heard this sort of thing before.

A sound site with invaluable information on good credit control and best payment practice. Information only, but a good portal to support groups.

www.paymentor.com
PayMentor

Overall rating: ★ ★ ★ ★			
Classification:	payment	**Readability:**	★ ★ ★ ★ ★
Updating:	occasionally	**Content:**	★ ★ ★ ★ ★
Navigation:	★ ★ ★ ★ ★	**Speed:**	★ ★ ★

UK   R

If you are a small business trying to survive despite unpaid invoices, the opening words of this site – 40% of invoices are unpaid after 60 days – will hit your Achilles' Heel. Founded by Louis Martin, who began a receivables management and debt collection company in Europe in the 1990s, it takes the logical step that debt collection should be more efficient over the Internet. As a subscriber to Paymentor, you have the benefit of an automatic 'invoice due for payment' reminder service and the follow-up service for the collection of late payments.

The site employs a full-time security expert and 24 hour network monitoring. Your business is allocated a Paymentor Agent.

A simple, logical site, it has a seriousness about it which makes one sure one wouldn't want to be on the receiving end of the service.

SPECIAL FEATURES

Product Demo is very slick, requiring a flash 4 plug in, which can be downloaded free from Macromedia via the site. Log in a name and enter the demo where the Paymentor system is explained. It pulls no punches outlining the effect late payment has on your business, then lists the stages it follows to chase your customers. These are:

Reminder Messages sent out before payment is due.

ResolvMentor settles invoice disputes before the payment is late.

Net-Collect is a timed, virtual debt collection tool via the Internet

WebCheq (after 40 days) is comprised of two stages: the first when only you can see the late payer. The second when details of the customer are shared with credit bureaux, who use the information as one of the criteria for their trade credit limits and credit rating.

AgentMentor gives details of seriously late paying customers to Paymentor's collection agents and lawyers.

At the login facility, connection is cut after 20 minutes without interaction to stop fraudulant invoices being entered under your name.

An excellent site and a very useful tool, especially for companies without a credit control department.

www.uk-debt-collection.co.uk
UK Debt Collection Service (Brittania Credit Recovery)

Overall rating: ★ ★ ★ ★			
Classification:	payment	**Readability:**	★ ★ ★ ★
Updating:	occasionally	**Content:**	★ ★ ★ ★ ★
Navigation:	★ ★ ★ ★	**Speed:**	★ ★ ★ ★

UK

This is one of two sites from the same Leeds-based company with similar content (see also www.britanniacredit.co.uk). Both sites are a shop window for the services offered, and requests for debt collection or business reports can be faxed, submitted online or by snail mail.

SPECIAL FEATURES

Services include debt collection, bailiff service, business reports on companies, credit vetting (on individuals and companies), legal services (for the issue of summons, process serving and pre-sue reports) and tracing absconders.

There is a smattering of features, including a useful one on credit control with practical advice.

Well-written with plenty of information about the companies activities. The online contact facility could save time and money.

OTHER SITES OF INTEREST

UK Debt Collection
www.ukdebtcollection.com

Alex Lawrie Factors
www.alexlawrie.com

financial advice

www.insolvency.co.uk
The Banking and Insolvency Website

Overall rating: ★ ★ ★ ★			
Classification:	information	**Readability:**	★ ★ ★ ★
Updating:	daily	**Content:**	★ ★ ★ ★
Navigation:	★ ★ ★ ★	**Speed:**	★ ★ ★ ★

UK

Though insolvency is an infinitely depressing subject, this is an intriguing site which hides its enormous resources in the most spartan layout imaginable. Ostensibly it's an information site on businesses for sale and in receivership, and there's a full list of UK liquidations and receiverships (archived back to 1996 when the site was set up) which covers Eire too. The list is very current, and the extent is horribly depressing. The site also provides general statistics on liquidations and receiverships, and companies in administration.

There is also a thorough listing of businesses for sale. Click on the brief description (type of business and annual turnover) for a more detailed description, and the administrators contact details.

SPECIAL FEATURES

Links are the site's strength, with listings of insolvency practitioners. You can search by firm, email, city, telephone number, and solicitors and barristers who specialise in insolvency and liquidation advice. There are further links to surveyors, auctioneers and valuers specialising in the disposal of liquidated stocks and assets, and the classified section is for advertising businesses for sale, and services and equipment required. Details can also be kept private. The system for posting messages is clear and well explained.

FAQs provide excellent general information on insolvency. Links to the DTI site lead to full details of the Insolvency Act 1996, and redundancy payment information. The other links here are brilliant, with direct access to the Lord Chancellor's Office, Official Receivers, the Courts, and advice listings about bankruptcy.

Coffee Break is hidden in the depths of the site, and is a must. Why one would come to this site for a coffee break facility defies explanation, but the links have to be seen to be believed. Whilst you are contemplating selling your business (or buying another one), you can find out the football results, link to shopping sites, computer magazines, universities, libraries, games, and software.

Professional covers courses and conferences, list practitioners, give legal updates, and access to the UK insolvency database.

The beauty of this site is the immense number of links it provides from the Government Stationary Office and Companies House to Arsenal Football Club and Sainsbury's. Unless you were a buyer, it's probably a site you hope you'll never have to visit, but worth bookmarking just for its portal resources.

www.unbiased.co.uk
Independent Financial Advisers

Overall rating: ★ ★ ★

Classification:	information	Readability:	★ ★ ★ ★ ★
Updating:	occasionally	Content:	★ ★ ★
Navigation:	★ ★ ★	Speed:	★ ★ ★

UK

This is the promotional vehicle for Independent Financial Advisers (IFAs) nation-wide, and serves a useful purpose for business looking for group pension advice, group life assurance and commercial mortgages. It's also a good starting place for the self-employed wanting advice on life assurance, income protection, critical illness cover, healthcare, tax planning, pensions, ISAs and equity release. The database, with details provided by the IFAs themselves, covers 9000, and you are linked by subject, postcode and preferred charging structure (fee v commission). You are also asked to supply your email address for IFA survey purposes. The number of employees in the firm is also requested.

SPECIAL FEATURES

Petition is an invitation to add your name to the protest that the IFA has set up against the imposition of multi-tied advisers (set up in April 2001). Browsers are asked to click on the signing link (you are linked to www.keepitindependent.co.uk). This page, however, is not a popup menu and you cannot return to the IFA home page.

IFA factsheets can be downloaded free, with Adobe Acrobat, and cover issues of personal financial planning and The Independent newspaper's Guide to Independent Financial Advice.

Press Releases are right up to date, and cover research commissioned by IFA Promotion.

Get Hector allows you to take out your frustrations on Hector the Tax Man. He is leaving the county and you have only ten chances to fire a bullet at his bowler hat to stop him absconding with billions in taxpayers money. Ok, so you should have better things to do, but everyone needs a break now and then. You will need the Flash 5 plug in.

Whatever the reason for your search for an IFA, this is the starting place to finding the right specialist in your area. Get trapped on the petition page, though, and you may be there for ever.

For more financial advice, see also the entries in Chapters One and Two, as many sites contain financial and tax advice for small businesses and sole traders.

legal advice

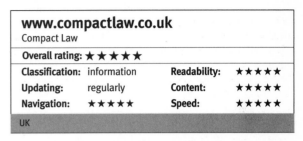

www.compactlaw.co.uk
Compact Law

Overall rating: ★ ★ ★ ★ ★			
Classification:	information	**Readability:**	★ ★ ★ ★ ★
Updating:	regularly	**Content:**	★ ★ ★ ★ ★
Navigation:	★ ★ ★ ★ ★	**Speed:**	★ ★ ★ ★ ★
UK			

You may have come across this one before in its previous guide as LawRights. For no apparent reason there has been a name change ('Compact' meaning binding agreement or understanding). This site claims to offer concise and independent legal information, as opposed to advice like the rest of its peer group, and was the first to offer a legal document service online.

Split between personal and business law, the document resources are comprehensive, making it a site well worth bookmarking. Though the tone is a bit impersonal (you have to dig to find out information about the Compact Law partners), it is highly professional and reassuringly well-informed.

SPECIAL FEATURES

Document Centre The documents available for business use cover commercial issues, Internet (which is excellent) and employment. Users of Microsoft Word 97 and 2000 can open a saved html document directly in word for editing or to save as template for use later. To buy a document, select the document form, and on the pop up window enter credit card details and your transaction is confirmed as complete. The document can then be opened as a new window. A transaction receipt will then be emailed to you. Prices for documents start at £12 to around £85.

Commercial Documents include agency agreement, confidentiality agreement, distribution agreement, joint ventures and a variety of partnership agreement templates. There is a selection of standard terms and condition templates too, for sale of goods and services. Free documents include agreement termination letters, change of notice address letter and letter before debt chasing action.

The Internet documents are excellent, and in variety some of the best around. It's a relatively new area and not well covered elsewhere. Areas include partnership agreements in various combinations, for sharing revenue and content supply, domain name agreements and website linking agreements. These templates are more expensive.

Employment Templates cover contracts in various forms, including flexible hours, but also cover the important area of internet and email use by employees both within the office and mobile workers. There are also policy documents on maternity and parental leave, sickness and absence.

There is plenty of free legal information within the site too, clearly laid out in a split column format. Accident claims, employment, injunctions, public funding and small claims court information will be most relevant to businesses.

CompactLaw Extras have articles on part-time worker regulations, National Minimum Wage, the Working Time Directive, Health and Safety at Work, with employment fact sheets and Q&A. Subjects covered here mainly concern unfair and wrongful dismissal, redundancy, discrimination, maternity rights and statutory sick pay.

As well as recommending some law books (mainly on divorce and the gentle art of negotiation), there is a keyword search link to Amazon.co.uk.

The County Court Fees information is very detailed, with information at the end of the page on situations in which you may not have to pay fees. The Civil Court Finder is split by regions.

Links are some of the best around. The 'useful sites' cover housing issues and are a motley selection, but the Government and organisation sites are almost faultless with some unexpected inclusions such as the Low Pay Commission, HSE, Land Registry, as well as obvious one like Companies House.

OTHER FEATURES

Top Ten Tips on consulting a lawyer are obviously written by lawyers and a bit dry, but useful nonetheless, and address of the Office for the Supervision of Solicitors and the Legal Services Ombudsman are also included. UK latest news is law news.

Helpline for legal questions is open from 8am-10pm – laudably long hours, and charged at £1.50 a minute. Information can also be accessed via a WAP enabled mobile phone.

Round of applause for a well laid out and easily navigable site. The links are especially good and the range of documents on offer should cover most people's requirements. Well deserving of five stars.

www.FirstLaw.co.uk
FirstLaw

Overall rating: ★ ★ ★ ★			
Classification: advice		Readability:	★ ★ ★
Updating: occasionally		Content:	★ ★ ★ ★
Navigation: ★ ★ ★ ★		Speed:	★ ★ ★ ★

UK R

FirstLaw was the first internet-only legal practice, set up in 2000, and it really has got the measure of the world wide web. To add to its credentials, the non-executive chairman is the vice president of the English Law Society.

Split between being a legal service for lay people and a partnership operating vehicle for lawyers, FirstLaw is a registration only site, but use the 'click here' link for an explanation of the legal tendering service the site offers. You email details of your legal enquiry, and FirstLaw will put your business out to tender to 400 law firms world-wide. It chooses ones with the expertise you need and invites them to compete for your work. The User Demo shows you how FirstLaw will contact you by phone to discuss your case then return a selection of quotes to you by email.

SPECIAL FEATURES

FirstLaw will place the law firm you are dealing with under contract, and remains in contact with you throughout the duration of your case. The tendering service is free, and the site claims to be impartial, though it receives a commission from the firm that you appoint.

A highly professional set up with all the credentials of a City law firm and regulated by the Law Society. An excellent time saver: FirstLaw takes the leg work out of shopping around for a competitive legal quote.

www.freelawyer.co.uk
Free Lawyer

Overall rating: ★ ★ ★ ★			
Classification: advice		Readability:	★ ★ ★ ★ ★
Updating: regularly		Content:	★ ★ ★ ★ ★
Navigation: ★ ★ ★ ★ ★		Speed:	★ ★ ★ ★ ★

UK

With justification, this site been voted one of the best on the internet. It dispels all the jokes about lawyers never doing anything for nothing. The site claims to contain one million words of legal text produced by solicitors, barristers and legal academics, and once you have put in your query in the search facility, a list of related files will appear via the Virtualawyer. Each area of expertise is covered by a lawyer whose face appears on the homepage (three men and three women – very PC), with a friendly 'Hello, I'm Mary, Robin, Matt ...' and so on.

The site is keen to point out that FreeLawyer is not a legal firm and does not give legal advice, just information, and that it cannot take the place of face to face consultation with a solicitor. For all that, though, it's a brilliant service, and though most of the information is on personal law (family, housing, consumer), there is a good section on employment law for employees and employers.

One gripe: a navigation icon does not appear until you have called up a list of files on a chosen subject. It gives you a site map to short cut the question section altogether and would be better if it was in evidence from the start.

SPECIAL FEATURES

Find a Solicitor's Firm and the **Legal Fee Estimates** section inter-link. Search for a legal specialist by town or postcode, then by area of law you need advice in. To receive an estimate you need to type in details of your query, which are then emailed to relevant experts. You can keep details on the 'My Case' page. The directory is in no way comprehensive – just one practice in the test town.

The Legal Services Plan was just that at the time of going to press – still on the drawing board. But Freelawyer has plans to link up with a leading insurance company to create a legal fees insurance, with an annual premium to cover certain legal fees. You can ask for details of developments to be emailed to your desk.

The Legal Café is a chatty page, with a Poll section on some issue unrelated to the law, UK news and site sponsors' links. The bulk of the page, though, is a Question and Answer feature. Queries cover consumer questions, but some feature employment law too. Here too you'll find reader's contributions and letters sent to the site.

Lawyers start the charging clock ticking the moment they shake hands with you, so this site is a godsend if you have a fairly straightforward legal query. As you would expect from lawyers the User Agreement is copious.

www.lawgym.com
Law Gym

Overall rating: ★ ★ ★ ★

Classification:	advice	Readability:	★ ★ ★ ★ ★
Updating:	regularly	Content:	★ ★ ★ ★
Navigation:	★ ★ ★ ★ ★	Speed:	★ ★ ★ ★ ★

UK   R   £   🔒

Originally VATad.com, this curiously named site comes from the question, is your business fit to compete? Unique amongst the virtual lawyer options, in that it offers advice and legal services exclusively to businesses, with the addition of company and commercial features written by accountants, entrepreneurs, and chartered tax advisers. Designed like a shopping site, you add options to your shopping basket.

Advice can be given online, over the phone or face to face, with the option of registering your query for their 'advice in one hour' option. Email advice comes in private files kept in a 128-bit encryption secure server, and each answer is insured up to £1.5 million. You pay on line or over the phone by credit card, and your 'account' is then open.

The site is designed in a neat little box, with all the pages appearing within the box. This fails to make use of the whole page, and text can appear very cramped, but somehow it is contained and reassuring. LawGym is nicely written and accessible, playing on the fact that lawyers can be stuffy and expensive, and with a web conference option in the pipeline, the site is set to meet FirstLawyer et al head on.

SPECIAL FEATURES

One Hour Advice Service appears to be unique on the web. Email your question, in less than 300 keyboard characters, and for £85 plus VAT paid by credit card, you will receive your reply within 60 minutes. For an additonal £30 plus VAT, a representative at LawGym will phone you.

12 Hour Advice is the cheaper option. Other services include telephone advice (you pay per 30 minutes), project advice, register a company, VAT reclaims, face to face advice (from £300 plus VAT for a half day), lawyer's letters and tax/VAT employment appeal representation.

Free PDF Downloads include company and commercial features (starting and running a business), employment law, protecting your business and business taxation. To view the options and download, you need to register by entering your email address.

Chat sounds complicated. Chats take place every third Wednesday of the month between 8 and 8.30pm. You submit a question, and discover if it has been selected by visiting the chat logon page. Topics chosen for discussion are posted by the second Wednesday of the month. LawGym claim this option is unique to them, which probably comes as no surprise!

Useful Links are unfortunately not always useful. Only one covers a business site, and LawGym would be better including business advice links, Inland Revenue and the like. The site lets itself down badly here.

Despite this hiccup, LawGym has a definite part to play in the burgeoning presence of lawyers on the web. Watch the fees – it may be cheaper in some cases to use a local lawyer face to face, who can see your relevant documents at short notice for a small fee.

www.lawontheweb.co.uk
Law on the Web

Overall rating: ★ ★ ★ ★			
Classification:	portal	**Readability:**	★ ★ ★ ★ ★
Updating:	regularly	**Content:**	★ ★ ★ ★
Navigation:	★ ★ ★	**Speed:**	★ ★ ★ ★ ★

UK

You'll want to bookmark this site as soon as you log on, just for the links to the other legal advice sites. It focuses on individual law issues, but some areas of the site and the sites mentioned (most of them reviewed here) cover business issues too. It's all big and brassy, but written in a friendly style.

However, on closer inspection it's not easy to navigate – the index is long and unwieldy, and you can find yourself in areas without knowing quite how you got there. Links aren't as great as they promise to be nor as comprehensive, so points lost as you delve further and further. Regular updating is promised though, so it's one worth keeping an eye on.

SPECIAL FEATURES

Legal Basics is where Law On the Web delivers its own legal information on business and employment issues. These are well presented though in an alarmingly large type size, with good listings , such as Employment Tribunal Offices.

Find a Lawyer is a directory that contains nearly 300 solicitors and 100 barristers' chambers, in a variety of specialities, which is one of the best legal directories on the web. The details were not complete when we visited, so it's anyone's guess how you are supposed to contact them. We are reliably informed that Law on the Web is in fact in the process of amending the entire directory system, which will result in just 100 web-friendly firms featuring in full on the site, with a link to the other major online legal directories

Free Legal Advice covers a mere handful of DIY law sites (like CompactLaw.co.uk, see p.55 for a review) and online document providing solicitors' forms. Law Online lists the online solicitors firms in various specialities, employment and debt collection being most relevant here.

Open Law claims to lists sites for legal work bids – you sit back and wait for the business to be tendered for – but sadly only one name appears.

Foreign Connections contains listings of law forms in 37 countries; reason enough to bookmark this site on your laptop when travelling. During boring moments you can dip into Law Fun (if it's possible to put those two words together?)

Legal Shop recommends law books (usually DIY ones) and links to Amazon.co.uk. The number of selected books is pretty good as are the Links, which go by category and there is a Site of the Week selected. Links are a curious element to include on the site which is all about links in the first place.

Full of information but harder to navigate than it first appears.

www.legal-advice-online.co.uk
Legal Advice Online

Overall rating: ★ ★ ★ ★			
Classification: advice		**Readability:**	★ ★ ★ ★ ★
Updating: occasionally		**Content:**	★ ★ ★ ★
Navigation: ★ ★ ★ ★ ★		**Speed:**	★ ★ ★ ★ ★

UK R

Hurrah! A site that tells you exactly what it is about right from the start. Somehow this clear and straightforward set up manages to communicate its message in one scroll down page. The result is that you understand quickly how to proceed and that's the job done. Though there is no mention of who the lawyers are behind the firm, there are pictures of the office entrances in London and Leeds (bit curious this), and you do have the feeling that this is no fly-by-night firm, but the real McCoy.

The legal advice service plays to the time element – you're too busy running a business to waste time visiting a lawyer's office - and claims to be 24 hours a day, which actually means that advice is given within 24 hours of receipt of payment. It may well be as it claims, for the picture at the top of the home page shows a dishevelled character who looks like he has been at his desk all night. The site is honest enough to admit that most issues can be resolved in one consultation. Click on Submission Form which asks questions about your query, and takes you to the payment option page (credit card or by cheque).

SPECIAL FEATURES

Legal Advice Online offers seven packages, ranging from the basic one at just under £40 to the most expensive at £249.99:

Basic Service offers a one-off email response to a problem or legal query and requests that you sent photocopies of relevant documents in advance of your query.

Silver Service is an annual fee which allows for one hour of legal work and six email enquiries.

Drafting Service is a letter writing option if you are owed money or receive a solicitor's letter yourself. The price includes a recorded delivery reply to the relevant individual or company and a follow-up phone call.

Document Checking Service includes all agreement issues such as leases, partnership agreements and business contracts, so long as the document is less than 2000 words (which isn't a great deal). You will also receive an email with discussion about any clauses which need your attention. More expensive is a drafting service, with charges per 250 words (again not a lot so take care you are not paying way over the odds).

Specialist Legal Packages can cover most subjects for just under £100 each. These are tailor made and updated, with relevant application forms and professionally drafted letters.

Internet Law Legal Service is the most expensive of the services offered, and covers instructions to web designers to limiting third party liability. This could be immensely useful for businesses setting up websites, who want to work with legal eagles in the business themselves.

Top marks for simplicity in a complicated world, but the costs look to be high, especially when compared to their competitors, or your local solicitor, so a charges comparison may be a good idea.

www.legalshop.co.uk
Legal Shop

Overall rating: ★ ★ ★ ★

Classification:	advice	Readability:	★ ★ ★ ★
Updating:	occasionally	Content:	★ ★ ★ ★
Navigation:	★ ★ ★ ★	Speed:	★ ★ ★ ★

UK R £

Sister site to FreeLawyer, Legal Shop provides fixed price advice on both business and personal legal matters. Like all good ideas it's simple and well put together. The three main areas covered are Fixed Price Legal Advice, Fixed Price Legal Services and Business Documents to buy. The tone of the site is convincing and professional – you'd feel confident coming here with a query.

SPECIAL FEATURES

Fixed Price Legal Advice Prices are listed down the left hand index and range from £25 to £85. You email your question, and a solicitor or barrister will reply, within three working days, with a document of between 500 and 750 words. The first step is to send your details to verify your identity – a legal requirement. To receive advice, browsers need to login which gives access to My Legal Shop for advice emailed back. There are examples of the style of replies.

Fixed Price Legal Services offers a range of pre-packaged legal services, delivered by a barrister or solicitor for a one-off fee.

Legal Representation comes from one of the lawyers listed in the Find A Law Firm section: searches are by postcode and area of law.

Business Documents for sale cover business, ecommerce and employment, and property, with prices starting at under

£10 for a Final Written Warning letter. Other subjects covered include contracts, non-disclosure documents, and disciplinary and grievance procedure.

Legal Advice Hotline is open for fixed price advice (£49.50) over the phone from 8am to 8pm Mon-Fri for business users (though there is an out-of-hours facility). Register your credit card details and you are allocated an 0800 number and (very long) order number.

A site well-deserving of the praise it has received. Excellent rates could save you a great deal of money, better spent that lining lawyers pockets. It would be nice to know who these virtual experts are though.

OTHER SITES OF INTEREST

solicitors Online
www.solicitors-online.com
The search facility of the Law Society Website. Search under speciality, solicitor's name, firm name, town, county or postcode for listing of specialist legal firms in your area. The site also gives details of dealing with solicitors and links to Lawyers For Your Business which gives access to 1300 business lawyers nationwide.

Lawyer Locator
www.lawyerlocator.co.uk
The find-a-lawyer directory of law resource centre Martindale-Hubble. Search by area of law, law firm name, postcode or town.

Connecting Legal
www.connectinglegal.com
Ostensibly a lawyers site, but with a directory of solicitors, barristers, accountants and surveyors world-wide.

Society of Financial Advisers
www.sofa.org
The Consumer section of the Society of Financial Advisers. SOFA offer the reassurance that members adhere to the organisations strict code of conduct. A simple set-up, the site offers two basic services: Financial advice, with features on why you should consult a financial adviser, what qualifications should you be looking for in one, what to do if you have problems and so on.

Legal Advice Free
www.legaladvicefree.co.uk
Legal advice free is exactly what you get, but this site is not nearly as comprehensive as some. Useful nonetheless for brief information on specific areas of business, especially finance and employment issues. The site offers advice, a directory of solicitors by county, quotes online for conveyancing and a questions forum.

Chapter 04

insurance & pensions

These are very important sites for businesses with employees, and for people who work alone who have dependants. Employers have obligations to ensure that they are adequately insured, yet an alarming number of businesses leave themselves open to catastrophe if the unthinkable was to happen to their computer system let alone to either an employee, a customer or the purchaser of a product they had merchandised.

Employers have also been obliged by law since October 2001 to provide a company pension if they employ more than five people. That legislation covers an enormous number of companies and partnerships which come under the small business umbrella. These sites can be utilised either to source and buy pensions online, and to keep abreast of pension and insurance regulations.

Libel insurance covering emails and internet content insurance is a very new area of the law, and this too is finding its way into insurance company websites.

For the self-employed person, the onus is on them to ensure that their insurance (both life and office) is adequate. For homeworkers especially, it is more than likely that office equipment and PCs are not covered by the household contents insurance, but there are insurance companies with good websites who specialise in these sort of policies. Life Assurance and pensions too are an important issue: can you be sure that your dependants would be provided for if you became unable to work, or your business and income was to die with you? The sites on insurance issues are good, which makes doing something about the future easier than ever.

information

www.abi.org.uk/consumer2
Association of British Insurers

Overall rating: ★ ★ ★			
Classification:	Information	Readability:	★ ★ ★ ★
Updating:	sporadically	Content:	★ ★ ★
Navigation:	★ ★ ★ ★	Speed:	★ ★ ★
UK			

Here you will find everything you want to know about insurance issues for small business and the self-employed. Go to Consumer on the main site index then Small Business, for two documents which cover all the essential details.

SPECIAL FEATURES

Insurance Advice for Small Businesses is a feature containing some sobering advice: 'Running a business creates considerable legal responsibilities ... Injury to your employees and members of the public could result in you being legally liable to pay damages if you or your employees have been negligent or found in breach of a statutory duty.'

Information covers income protection, personal accident or sickness, life assurance and pensions. It then spells out the role of insurance companies, brokers, and other intermediaries. There's advice too on protecting against fire, theft, vandalism, weather damage and arson. A second feature gives guidelines on protecting laptop computers from theft, with useful addresses and the ABI's own video and information sheet.

A great starting point for new businesses or these newly self-employed when they come to consider insurance.

www.adviceonline.co.uk
AdviceOnline Ltd

Overall rating: ★ ★ ★ ★			
Classification:	Insurance	Readability:	★ ★ ★ ★
Updating:	regularly	Content:	★ ★ ★
Navigation:	★ ★ ★	Speed:	★ ★ ★
UK			

AdviceOnline is the internet arm of the Berg Kaprow Lewis Group of Independent Chartered Accountants, and advice is given via its associated company, Park Row Associates Plc based in London and around the UK.

As well as financial advice, insurance and pensions, the site also offers lending services and direct investment, including online sharetrading (with imiweb.co.uk). Most useful perhaps for the self-employed, there is information and advice for employer's stakeholder pensions, which confusingly, comes from Pensionsbusiness.com (see p.64).

Browsers can use the Direct Offer Services, a sort of self-select, self-service system with no specific client advice, but the site stresses that policies may not have the necessary cover.

Alternatively, use the Advice Services which involves filling in a detailed Fact Find questionnaire, a Financial Services Act requirement. Initial advice is free of charge (either emailed, by phone or face to face) until you select a policy, then you decide whether to pay a fee or commission.

SPECIAL FEATURES

Quotation Centre covers level term insurance, decreasing term insurance, pension term assurance, critical illness assurance, family income benefit, whole of life assurance and personal health insurance. For example, Life Assurance gives you the option of cheapest quote (immediate online with no advice for term, mortgage protection and family income benefit only or with a personal quote search which takes 24 hours). You are required to read the Park Row Associates Terms of Business letter before completing a quick or full personal information questionnaire. The questionnaire page was unavailable at time of writing.

Interesting Articles are really information documents on subjects such as stakeholder pensions and life assurance. These are fairly simple and clear. More complicated however are the pension audit calculator and personal tax and NI calculator (under Planning Tools).

General Insurance covers car insurance and breakdown cover, both via external sites, quotesystem.co.uk and vehicle-breakdown-cover.co.uk respectively.

AdviceOnline makes life complicated for itself with heavy going navigation, and you often find yourself back at the same page via a different route. The home page, which shows market prices, could do with a better explanation of the aims of the site. It's frustrating unless you know exactly what you are looking for.

www.directlife.co.uk
Direct Life & Pension Services

Overall rating: ★ ★ ★ ★			
Classification: Insurance		**Readability:**	★ ★ ★ ★
Updating: regularly		**Content:**	★ ★ ★ ★
Navigation: ★ ★ ★ ★		**Speed:**	★ ★ ★
UK			

The online arm of Direct Life and Pension Services, independent financial advisers, this site deals with personal insurance and pensions, which are essential for the self-employed, and those without a company pension plan.

DirectLife has a stable of big league insurance companies from which it can obtain immediate quotes (including names like Standard Life, Norwich Union, Royal and Sun Alliance, and Legal & General), but from this initial stage you are left to your own devices. You can ask to be sent application forms, and supply your name and address details.

Company Information lists the terms and conditions of the site. Here there are disclaimers such as 'The nature of the technology means that the quotes system cannot be guaranteed. Terms are therefore only deemed to form a 'contract' when a proposal is completed and an acceptance letter issued by the insurer.'

SPECIAL FEATURES

Quotes and Product Information Product Guides is the most useful section with good explanations about life cover, critical illness cover, level term insurance, waiver of premium and special policies such as:

Life Plus: which includes a level of life insurance, usually paid on diagnosis of terminal illness, specified at outset and guaranteed to remain constant for the term of the plan, with the addition to and totally independent of the life cover, a level amount of critical illness cover set at a fixed percentage of the life cover amount at outset guaranteed to remain constant for the term of the plan.

Mortgage Plus: which includes a level of life insurance specified at outset, usually paid on diagnosis of terminal illness, which reduces at a rate to match the reducing capital balance on a typical repayment mortgage. Plus, the plan also includes an amount of critical illness cover, totally independent of the life cover, set at a fixed percentage of the life cover amount and which is guaranteed to remain at a fixed percentage of the life cover for the term of the plan.

On completion of the online application form (with vague questions on topics such as age, term of insurance, joint policy details, smoker), a handful of quotes appear very swiftly. Once you have selected those you are interested in, you then complete your address details for applications to be sent to you by snail mail.

Information on Stakeholder Pensions is thorough, with a good pension calculator, but applications can still only be made by calling a freephone number, despite their announcement in the Q & A section that states they will be offering an online Stakeholder pension service from 2001. The site is adamant that it is giving no advice on the products suitability and advises you to seek expert advice before buying a pension.

Excellent information on the details of various types of cover, and good starting point for whittling down quotes, but policy details are non-existent. The cheapest quote may not be providing adequate cover. Follow up research is at the applicant's risk.

www.insurancewidebiz.com/business

InsuranceWide.com Services. Ltd

Overall rating: ★ ★ ★ ★			
Classification:	Insurance	Readability:	★ ★ ★ ★
Updating:	regularly	Content:	★ ★ ★ ★
Navigation:	★ ★ ★ ★	Speed:	★ ★ ★

UK

A UK-based, multi-product online insurance channel, InsuranceWide.com is a joint venture between insurance and online operators including Freeserve PLC, GlobalNet Financial.com PLC, Cox Insurance Holdings PLC and Harrison Son Hill & Co. Ltd. It provides a wide range of insurance policies covering motor, home, travel and life insurance, but there is a special business page which covers all areas of business insurance.

All policies are sourced from a selection of leading UK authorised insurance companies, many of which (it is claimed) have never previously been made available for purchase online. Companies are premier league and include AXA, Cornhill, CPP Card Protection, Equity Red Star, Hiscox, Lloyds, Norwich Union, Provident, Royal & Sun Alliance, Scottish Provident, Trenwick International and Zurich Insurance. The site doesn't put your business out to bids. It acts more as a portal and links you to the insurer who deals with that area.

Under each business area there is a brief column of text outlining why you need to be insured and the particular areas which need careful attention. Interesting insurable inclusions are Web Monitoring and Cyber Liability (insurance against infringement of intellectual property rights, breach of confidence or infringement of any right to privacy, misuse of any information which is either confidential or subject to statutory restrictions on its use, defamation, and inadvertent transmission of a virus). Ironically this area is not yet insurable online via the site however.

Browsers should read the Site Info Page which, it will come as no surprise to discover, is as long as your arm and details how you should proceed when dealing with individual insurance companies. You are advised to read the separate privacy statement or policy 'on the particular site which applies to the use by the insurance provider concerned of the information collected on that site'.

All links to insurance products are via secure channels, so that when you request a quotation or apply to purchase an insurance policy online, your personal information is transmitted in encrypted form.

The site is scattered with little boxes which start with doom laided scenarios – 'What would you do if...'. Add to this the nature of the advice given under each area of business, and you will be in such a state, you'll be insuring yourself against the sun not rising tomorrow. But the list of top notch insurers the site employs gives it a certain gravitas, and for the basic information and ease of links is worthwhile using to obtain quotes.

www.moneyextra.com
MoneyExtra

Overall rating: ★ ★ ★ ★

Classification:	Insurance	Readability:	★ ★ ★ ★
Updating:	daily	Content:	★ ★ ★ ★
Navigation:	★ ★ ★ ★	Speed:	★ ★ ★

UK

With a remit to provide impartial advice from the widest selection of providers, MoneyExtra should probably sit in the financial advice chapter. However, with subjects covered including homebuying, loans and cards, savings best buys and home/travel and motor insurance, most is aimed at personal finance issues. It finds itself here because the compare and buy facility of the life and illness insurance section, the tax tables in the budgeting and tax section, and the latest annuity rates of the pension section are most useful to small businesses.

The basic site index covers compare and buy (this does not include pensions), a good news and features section (with archived features, daily stock report and stock report archive), and guides and tools.

MoneyExtra is a subsidiary of Bristol and West and gets its information from a first rate list of sources (including FTSE, MoneyFacts and Price Waterhouse Coopers). It tries hard to be a comprehensive information provider, but it has its frustrations. The tax tables listing covers almost everything, but there was no joy when we tried to glean information on corporation tax and company car tax.

SPECIAL FEATURES

Pensions and Retirement is split into FAQs and guides and tools. The former covers the full gamut from why one type of pension would suit to information about stakeholder pensions for employers. The latter offers a tax relief on pensions chart, and a pensions glossary, with jargon busting. The Quick Links take you to questions such as tax relief for the self-employed and the latest pension news and features. Not the sexiest of news items, but the information is clear and concise.

Budgeting and Tax has invaluable charts to compare tax rates (despite the glitches already mentioned). There's a jargon busting glossary here too, plus personal tax calculator, economic forecast feature and features on budgeting for school fees (not really a small business concern but well written), and finance for women – but the gremlins wouldn't give access here either.

Life and Health Cover is more satisfactorily interactive with a good insurance rates comparison. Guides include explanations on level term assurance, decreasing term assurance, income protection, critical illness cover, family income benefit and mortgage payment protection. Rate facts come from MoneyFacts, and to complete the quote inquiry you have to provide names.

OTHER FEATURES

The site offers a financial services team helpline with advice from independent financial advisors, open 9 to 6.30 weekdays, with a call-back facility.

Almost there with a healthy combination of information and comparison tables. No accounting for the glitches in information provision, but frustrating and most of them were relevant to small business.

www.pensionbusiness.com
The Stakeholder Pension Company Ltd

Overall rating: ★ ★ ★ ★			
Classification:	Pensions	**Readability:**	★ ★ ★ ★
Updating:	regularly	**Content:**	★ ★ ★ ★
Navigation:	★ ★ ★ ★	**Speed:**	★ ★ ★

UK R

A simple idea executed in a straightforward way and far less complicated than AdviceOnline which has a direct link to this site (see p.64).

Pensionbusiness.com is a member of DBS Financial Management Plc, and describes itself as ' a straightforward alternative for employers wanting to put in place a stakeholder pension scheme for their company online'. The emphasis is on speed, efficiency and security. It would take a brave director to plunge in with no contact with the company providing the selected policy, and the site does stress that its Direct Offers do not carry advice and it's advisable to consult a financial adviser.

SPECIAL FEATURES

The site has links with big pension providers, including Legal & General, Scottish Mutual, Norwich Union, Clerical Medical and Scottish Amicable. Once you have made your selection, pensionbusiness.com will provide an online employee service (who will receive packages about the selected plan and can use an assigned username and password to access the company pension details on the site.) It will also help with pension admin and the deduction of employee contributions from the payroll.

The Employers Start Here listing in the index leads you by the hand through the application process, starting with reasons why you need a top quality pension scheme in place and how those with more than five employees are obliged by law to offer a pension from October 2001. Run the mouse icon over the five important facts and a pop-up box appears padding out the information. There is more detailed information about stakeholder, occupational and group personal pension schemes.

Once you investigate the products, you enter the secure area of the site, and as you move the cursor over the details of each companies pension policies (payment method, company name, investment strategy) more details appear in a pop-up box. Clicking on underlined words takes you to more information about the product. Once you have selected the pension most suitable to you, you are requested to fill in company details and complete the application form.

The beauty of this site is in the ease with which you can sign up your company to a pension plan. It's the internet at its best and all sounds too good to be true, so it's worth taking the sites own advice that you request further details about each plan.

www.pensions-online.co.uk
IFA Online Ltd

Overall rating: ★ ★ ★ ★ ★			
Classification:	Pensions	Readability:	★ ★ ★ ★
Updating:	regularly	Content:	★ ★ ★ ★
Navigation:	★ ★ ★ ★	Speed:	★ ★ ★ ★

UK £

No messing here. A minimalist site, giving independent financial advice 100% over the internet, but which rather coyly admits to being the first to do so in the UK. Established in 1997, IFA Online Ltd is based in Nottingham and is part of the Burns-Anderson Independent Network Plc.

SPECIAL FEATURES

Best Buys provides details of different pension providers, highlighting those which offer best value for money personal pensions on the basis of charges, performance and administration. Click on the criteria of companies (not comprehensive but selected by charging, structure and flexibility) and performance (rated by Micropal Standard & Poors', against its peer groups, five points meaning fund is in the top 20%) and then, once you have selected a provider, click 'apply', which is an email process.

Advice provides fee-based financial advice, recommended for those about to part with large contributions, business owners or those about to purchase an annuity. Completion and submission of the pension enquiry form costs £200 before you receive any advice, and the minimum fee is £350, in addition to the fees charged by the product provider, though any initial commission paid to IFA Online is refunded in the form of a rebate to your plan.

OTHER FEATURES

Guides is simply a link to Adobe documents from the Department of Social Security on all types of pensions, including those for the self-employed, stakeholder pensions, occupational pensions, and pensions for women.

The Calculator is for working out how much you need to contribute to your pension to make sure your retirement is going to be comfortable. Fill in your age and age of retirement, and income. Inflation rate, investment return and annuity rate are supplied, but can be adjusted and helpful advice pops up in the Help box on rates marked with '?'. Completion advice is straight from the hip: 'use only numbers or it won't work'!

Bearing in mind financial advice can be commission based from an IFA, IFA Online's fees appear to be steep, but the information is valuable, and right at your fingertips. Not the best in its category but worth a look.

OTHER SITES OF INTEREST

Tolson Messenger
www.tolsonmessenger.co.uk
Tolson Messenger is unique in that it is an on and offline London-based insurance company specialising in cover for home workers and small businesses as well as dealing with risk management, corporate insurance, personal insurance and providing independent financial advice through Tolson Messenger Financial Services Ltd. Worth a look for comparing quotes against other major insurance companies. Despite a quirky design, the information is easy to find and to follow, and the About Us information shows the company to be genuine.

UK Insurance Driectory
www.uk-insurance-directory.com
First stop site for searching for UK insurers in 26 categories. Much of the site is for domestic insurance purposes, but many business sectors are covered, including business, commercial, computer, credit, home, income protection, legal protection, liability, livestock, medical, travel, and musical instruments. Simply select the area you are interested in at the top of the page, or choose from the drop down menu. Links to relevant sites are then revealed.

See also many of the sites mentioned in Chapter One which give insurance and pensions advice.

Chapter 05

employment & training

Taking on staff is a quantum leap for most businesses. It's a symbol of expansion, and brings with it a raft of responsibilities and obligations. These can be checked out both on the sites mentioned in this chapter and in those in chapter four and chapter seven, which cover Government websites.

Finding staff is often difficult for businesses too small to employ an HR specialist, and too busy to spend the time trawling recruitment agencies or placing expensive advertising. It's not a problem for which the internet has yet found a solution. We are not entirely convinced about the success of the recruitment companies. These websites appear to be for the most part an advertisement for the agencies, and contact needs to be made by phone. This is not surprising when staffing involves personal contact and the right chemistry, but it's early days. We foresee that

initial contact and presentation of CVs will happen more and more online. Who knows? We might even end up with virtual staff!

But with staff come problems, and employers need to be fully aware what their and their employees' rights are when it comes to disciplinary proceedings. These matters are handled very well, especially in sites like ACAS (see p.72), and Equality Direct (p.74).

Training sites can be of particular use to sole proprietors, as well as employers looking to keep their staff's skills up-to-speed. Online learning (a subject close to the government's heart at the moment; see chapter seven) is moving on apace, and, with a wide variety of business skills covered, it represents all that is inspirational about the web.

www.acas.org.uk
Advisory, Conciliation and Arbitration Service

Overall rating: ★ ★ ★ ★ ★

Classification:	arbitration	Readability:	★ ★ ★ ★ ★
Updating:	regularly	Content:	★ ★ ★ ★ ★
Navigation:	★ ★ ★ ★ ★	Speed:	★ ★ ★ ★

UK

ACAS was mentioned daily on the news during the 1980s when the unions were at war with the Government. In fact the service, funded by the tax payer, is used most often by small businesses who do not have a personnel department. In 1999 they apparently dealt with 1500 requests to resolve disputes.

The site is excellent, in an area which could be bogged down in employment jargon. It's light and easy to read, with plenty of information for employers and employees who want to know their rights, as well as a resource for when negotiations get sticky. The tone of the site, especially in the About Us section, is approachable and friendly – a calm presence when employment issues become heated.

The main index covers employment topics, with a pop up menu of Tips for Workers who have Employment Problems, and has a comprehensive list of subjects including recruitment, employment policies and rights, communications in the workplace, and relations between employee and employer. Click on each heading for more detailed information in each area. The Q&A section includes examples of the 750,000 plus enquiries ACAS has each year.

SPECIAL FEATURES

Employment Topics within this section check out Keeping Up to Date for latest news bulletins free from ACAS. With the news section, browsers can subscribe to an email alert service which immediately informs you when ACAS posts news on its site.

Contact Us lists the telephone numbers and addresses of the ACAS telephone helpline, run from 11 offices nationwide.

Publications can be downloaded free by installing Acrobat reader from the Abode website link. These include publications on these topics (all of which are featured under Employment Topics) though some are available as handbooks and booklets:

• Recruitment and starting work
• Employment polices and practices
• Working together for success: the ACAS Standard
• Communications in the workplace
• Employment rights
• Problems between individuals and employers
• Relations between employers and employee representatives

The site also lists details of ACAS workshops and events around the country, which average about seven each month, with information about how to book by phone.

ACAS Quiz is useful if you have nothing better to do (or your conciliation negotiations have come to a stalemate). It asks fun questions on good practice, know your rights, about ACAS and trivia. The latter asks questions such as 'what is the most popular meal eaten during conciliation meetings?' Now you can't resist looking at the site can you?

An excellent site, which is actually fun to read. Invaluable not just for conciliation purposes, but for general employment law and rights information. Not a subject you would imagine had much to make you smile.

www.brookstreet.co.uk
Brook Street

Overall rating: ★ ★ ★			
Classification:	recruitment	Readability:	★ ★ ★ ★
Updating:	daily	Content:	★ ★ ★ ★
Navigation:	★ ★ ★ ★	Speed:	★ ★ ★ ★

UK

The website of one of the oldest office recruitment companies in the UK. Brook Street deals mainly with office, accounting and light industrial employment, both permanent and temporary. Split into two sections: job seekers and employers, this is the portal site to the local branch web pages. Search by postcode and you have access to available jobs in your area. Employers can register for temporary or permanent staff online, and post their requirements online, and are allocated a Consultant from the nearest branch. Payment is on results.

SPECIAL FEATURES

Jobseekers covers CV writing and interview techniques. Though aimed at fairly low-grade jobs, anyone would do well to read them. There's help too with returning to work, and details of Brook Street's Advantage system, a PC-based assessment to grade skills which all applicants have to undergo.

Very simple and easy to navigate. An ideal way to apply for jobs online or find staff.

www.thebiz.co.uk
Business Information Zone

Overall rating: ★ ★ ★ ★			
Classification:	directory	Readability:	★ ★ ★ ★
Updating:	regularly	Content:	★ ★ ★ ★
Navigation:	★ ★ ★ ★	Speed:	★ ★ ★ ★ ★

UK

Another business website which could fit into any chapter in this book, but it's here because it's resources on employment, training and recruitment are excellent. TheBiz is probably the premier online UK business to business information resource, with an extensive directory of companies covering not just employmen,t but business hardware and services, cars, computing, dispatch, financial, information services, internet, marketing, and travel.

To use, just select the sector in which you want to find a company; your choice is refined and then once you have made your selection, a list of relevant companies appears. If you are stumped or can't find the right peg for the right hole, the Directory of Directories offers a search service (answer within 24 hours), and a links to several search engines.

OTHER FEATURES

TheBiz lists business events (by organiser, sector, date and venue), and training information. There is also an extensive forum where you can post requests for financial backing, help with a new venture, businesses for sale, and seek or give advice on issues such as HR, sales, and technology.

Register Company allows you the opportunity to include your company in the directory.

TheBiz is the biz; straightforward, with plenty of information as promised. One to bookmark.

www.equalitydirect.org.uk
Equality Direct

Overall rating: ★ ★ ★ ★			
Classification:	employment	**Readability:**	★ ★ ★
Updating:	regularly	**Content:**	★ ★ ★ ★
Navigation:	★ ★ ★ ★	**Speed:**	★ ★ ★ ★
UK			

Set up by DLA, the international law firm and the charity, Broadcast Support Services, Equality Direct is designed to give employers and managers advice on equality issues in the workplace. This is the only website to advertise a free and confidential advice line to experts (open every day at the local call), but the site itself is a useful resource for employment information. The partners behind the service are excellent; the Small Business Service, ACAS, Federation of Small Businesses, Commission for Racial Equality, Equal Opportunities Commission, Disability Rights Commission, Department of Education and Employment and the DTI, and the online advice is thorough and authoritative.

Certain areas of the site are still under construction at time of writing, including the latest news link, and you'll be challenged to find out information about Promotion Issues and Practices. But the bones of the site are there, and most areas have been fleshed out, with the option of a low graphics browser. As there is no advertising on the site, one assumes revenue comes from the supporting partners.

The online features are listed in an index down the left column of the page, with the aim of telling employers what the law says about equality in the workplace, and how good polices and practices can be introduced effectively to suit your company.

Click on the Accessing the Web link on the right hand side of the page for information on adjusting your browser to make the site more readable. The layout however is clear and easy to follow, and the only gripe is the rather stilted language, steeped in employment law verbage.

SPECIAL FEATURES

Getting the Right People offers advice on good recruitment practice.

Building Your Business explains the basics of being an employer.

Is it Working? advises you on monitoring and what to do when it all goes pear-shaped.

Making the Most of Your Investment gives guidelines on preparing an equality policy for your company. The features themselves are clear with plenty of bullet points and subheadings, and the Topic Overview enables you to jumped ahead and around the subject.

Contact Us is more than just an email link. There is a clear explanation about the site's aims, and some good links to other useful sites.

This is one that all new employers should look at. Most effective because it brings together in one site the issues on the sites of all the partners – all reviewed elsewhere in this book. Narrowly misses the five star rating because it could do with more information about the elusive 'advisers' on the end of the helpline.

www.learndirect.co.uk
Learn Direct

Overall rating: ★ ★ ★ ★			
Classification: training		**Readability:**	★ ★ ★ ★
Updating: weekly		**Content:**	★ ★ ★ ★
Navigation: ★ ★ ★ ★		**Speed:**	★ ★ ★

UK

Very New Labour, Learn Direct was set up in response to the Government's Green Paper 'The Learning Age' as a vehicle for people to learn new skills and for businesses to improve their competitiveness.

The site is run by UFI (University for Industry), with Government backing, with a mission statement to 'stimulate and meet the demand for lifelong learning'.

The idea is that you can use the website to search for a relevant course, then contact your local Learn Direct call centre (1000 round the country), who will enrol you to complete the course at the centre, online or where courses are available at national and local colleges. Businesses might be better suited to accessing the courses online, which involves enrolling at a virtual learning centre. It all sounds complicated, but the helpline number takes you through to your nearest centre and they can point you in the right direction.

From the wheel icon on the home page, select an area from the choice of Getting Started, Find a Course, Get that Job, Build Your Business and Who can Help?

SPECIAL FEATURES

Find A Course covers the learning areas: Automotive, Basic Skills, Business and Management, Environmental Services and Technology, Information Technology, Multimedia and Retail and Distribution. As an example, Business Management offers 357 courses on a wide variety of topics such as appraisal interviewing, giving presentations, improving safety, Kaizen (the Japanese Business technique) or preparing a budget. Some courses are PC only, though there are promises that they will become MAC compatible.

Prices for the courses are not available online, to encourage you to contact a Learn Direct centre and because prices vary depending on any financial support learners may be able to receive.

Build Your Business has an extensive course catalogue under subject headings of Finance, HR, IT, Law, Marketing and Strategy. Click on the button for a full list under each heading. Law, for example, deals with discrimination, equal opportunities, harassment, improving safety and Health and Safety. Finance courses offer basic budgeting skills and understanding balance sheets, to more advanced techniques with cashflow and managing working capital. There are factsheets available as an overview, and a course taster: simply select the type of trader or manager you are from the drop down menu, and a selection of taster courses will be offered. Within each course there is a Check My Understanding revision facility, just to ensure you have been concentrating.

Who Can Help? Provides solutions to obstacles in taking the courses, with advice on childcare options, disability, and paying for learning, with links to the Individual Learning Account Website and other funding sources.

Latest News advertises the new 24 hour Learner Services helpline (for those who have no childcare and are at the PC in the wee small hours once the kids are in bed?)

OTHER FEATURES

From the homepage, the site highlights a course of the week (spreadsheets at time of writing) with an overview of the course, plus a learner profile as a promotion for the courses one supposes.

Like many Government-backed websites, the tone of Learn Direct is friendly and supportive. 'You can do it and we can help'. An excellent resource for small companies which cannot offer employees/managers the opportunity to take courses, and a good starting point for new business people who need to brush up or start from scratch with basic business skills.

The following websites deal with regional equality issues:

NORTH EAST:

Equality North East
http://www.equality-ne.co.uk

NORTH WEST:

Equality North West
http://www.equality.org.uk

SOUTH EAST:

SE Equality
http://www.seequality.org.uk

YORKSHIRE AND HUMBERSIDE:

Biznet
http://www.biznet.org/index.html

www.manpower.co.uk & www.gojobsite.co.uk
Manpower

Overall rating: ★ ★ ★ ★			
Classification:	recruitment	Readability:	★ ★ ★ ★
Updating:	regularly	Content:	★ ★ ★ ★
Navigation:	★ ★ ★ ★	Speed:	★ ★ ★ ★

UK

Though these two sites are independent – Manpower has less emphasis on recruitment online – they work together.

The Manpower site ostensibly advertises its client services and further information about recruitment can be gained by email or by the office locator. The site also promotes the virtues of Manpower's training facilities.

Gojobsite is the online recruitment part of the partnership, and deals with 35 different industry sectors. Split between Job Hunters and Clients, as a potential employer your job can be emailed to job hunters registered with the site, advertised as a display ad and listed in the corporate pages of the site.

Manpower has a superior site in terms of resources, but without the online recruitment facility. Gojobsite's boast of 100,000 jobs advertised each month must be worth further investigation.

www.oneclickhr.com
OneClickHR

Overall rating: ★ ★ ★			
Classification:	HR online	Readability:	★ ★ ★ ★
Updating:	regularly	Content:	★ ★ ★ ★
Navigation:	★ ★ ★	Speed:	★ ★ ★

UK   R

Originally OneClickHR produced software solutions, but in 2000 this site was established as a 'one stop virtual HR department' enabling companies to manage their HR admin online. Services offered include pre-employment health checks, payroll processing, the latest HR news, employment law advice online, psychometric testing and online training. The company is listed on the London AIM.

The site is busy, busy, so the best option is to select your company type (small, intermediate, corporate) from the zones index. You are then given an index of the services on offer. For small businesses, these include recruitment, health management, employment information management and termination of employment. The latter includes a disciplinary employment letter package and employment advice online. Once you have decided OneClickHR can help you, you register and are allocated an account number.

The company has a call back facility if you would rather make contact by phone; in the interactive 'zone' there is a poll and a discussion forum too for airing your views.

SPECIAL FEATURES

Products and Services The meat of the site is in this directory found on the right-hand column of the homepage. Once you have selected the document you need – the choice covers a wide variety of employment issues in detail – you fill in your account details and download the document.

Documents updated within 12 months due to legislative changes can be brought again for just £10.

OneClickHR also offers a complete HR outsourcing facility, though once again this gem is hidden in the busy index of icons.

OneClickBenefits is under construction, but will become a financial advice facility in partnership with Thomson Benefit Consultants offering free pensions advice, presentations and employee packages. Commission is paid by the company you choose to buy your pension from.

Recommended Links is actually an advertising vehicle and many of the categories have one or no entries – as yet.

OneClickHR is confident and assertive. The site could do with some housekeeping, and its benefits are not immediately obvious, but worth digging around to find the good stuff.

www.reed.co.uk
Reed Recruitment

Overall rating: ★ ★ ★			
Classification:	recruitment	**Readability:**	★ ★ ★
Updating:	daily	**Content:**	★ ★ ★ ★
Navigation:	★ ★ ★	**Speed:**	★ ★

UK   R

Another of the big recruitment agencies, but Reed's site is slow and unwieldy. You might have filled your vacancy by the time the right page loads. Having said that, Reed has a lot to offer. The emphasis is on job hunters (more so than its competitors), but the client services are extensive, with learning resources, advertising campaign management, assessments, Ecruitment (has that word found its way into the OED?), executive search, graduate recruitment, HR outsourcing and consultancy, training and, oh yes, recruitment. (This list is not exhaustive.)

Select the area of interest from the drop down menu, to receive more information about them, but contact is by telephone, text chat or via the nearest branch initially. Once you have posted a recruitment ad, jobs are emailed or texted to candidates daily, and are viewable by WAP phone or PDAs.

A big site for a big company. Not the easiest to follow, but worth sticking with.

www.tiger.gov.uk
Tiger (Department of Trade & Industry)

Overall rating: ★ ★ ★			
Classification:	information	Readability:	★ ★ ★ ★
Updating:	regularly	Content:	★ ★ ★ ★ ★
Navigation:	★ ★ ★ ★	Speed:	★ ★ ★ ★

UK

A government site which has sneaked in here from Chapter 7. However this is its rightful place, as TIGER is a clever acronym, thought up by a civil servant in Whitehall somewhere, for Tailored Interactive Guidance on Employment Law.

Linked to the DTI, this is the user-friendly resource for employees and employers to check up on their situation and rights in law. The bare bones are all there is at the moment (more of a cub than a tiger?), as the site is under construction, but it's looking good and should be worth keeping an eye on.

At the time of writing, there are links to the DTI and UK Online, and an index covering National Minimum Wage, Maternity Rights and Employment Relations (the latter links straight through to the DTI site itself). Maternity information is as yet only available to employees, but NMW details are fuller: split between employee and employer. For the employer there is a 'decision tree' with information on worker eligibility, rules and an NMW reckoner.

Still in its infancy, but cuts through civil service jargon to deliver information in a very user-friendly way.

www.trainingzone.co.uk
Training Zone

Overall rating: ★ ★ ★ ★			
Classification:	information	Readability:	★ ★ ★ ★ ★
Updating:	occasionally	Content:	★ ★ ★ ★
Navigation:	★ ★ ★ ★	Speed:	★ ★ ★ ★

UK   R

At first this site is a bit of a visual porridge, with a plethora of information bombarding your senses. A flashing box encourages you to join the TrainingZone free – and promises you'll never see the flashing icon again, which is all the encouragement we needed. But that's not the only reason for joining: membership gives you access to even more areas of this excellent site which positively bursts with information and resources. For members there is Newswire access, a Company Information Zone, a 30 day free Newsfeed (3500 stories each day if you're pushed for things to do), and a shopping online facility for accountancy publications, software, training and marketing products.

The A-Z site guide is the best starting place for a run down of the goodies on offer and it's not unlike a box of chocolates. You find something that's ideal, and scroll down again and hey presto! there's something even better. The site manages to include features and direct you to other sites for more detailed information in certain sectors. One quibble: some of these links do not appear as pop-up boxes.

SPECIAL FEATURES

Resources The emphasis of the site is on training and the resources here are practically perfect. Find links for training online, product suppliers, venues, and courses. The Experts' Guide has a good list of 'how to' features for trainers from starting out, to costing services, and getting accredited.

CareerZone includes a job search (including four top jobs posted each month) and a vacancy posting facility, and an opportunity to tender for training or consultancy work. The Leaning Campus enables you to find or create a learning event, plus there are some useful government site links.

News and Info has up-to-date training and development info, and a Newswire archive for topic searches.

A-Z index Scroll down and the site produces much more than just training info. You'll find a lawyer search (claiming to be the largest in the country with 54,000 listed) plus tips on briefing a solicitor; meeting and conference venues with over 200 listed; a link to the Sift CPD Business School; payroll services online; women in the workplace, with a link to the Women and Equality Website and good employment information and links to www.j4b.co.uk, the business grants site.

Freelancers Advice Centre deserves special mention, with an excellent feature on freelancing, working chronologically through the processes of going freelance and highlighting issues like IR35, with links to BusinessLink, BT, the Inland Revenue and banks amongst others.

TrainingZone majors on a specialist theme each month – at time of writing, management development was featured.

The Discussion Forum is lively with the opportunity to answer members' questions, participate in surveys and join in a Tuesday lunchtime discussion online.

TrainingZone claims to be the most popular site in the UK for trainers and HR professionals with 32,000 members. Packed with information not just for those interested in giving or receiving training. It's a great portal for information on starting up, accountancy, tax issues, going freelance, employing staff, finding a job...see for yourself.

equipment & software

Computers, phones, mobiles, palm pilots, PDAs, WAP phones. It can be impossible to do business without them, but the same items can cause serious inconvenience if you're not buying the best model for your needs. The drawback of shopping for anything online is that there is no chance to suck it and see. Before we part with cash, whether it be for a single PC or for a complete office telephone system, we all like to know what it is we are buying.

There is a vast array of hardware, software and equipment suppliers, many with offline shops and some which only trade on the internet. There are two options here: either buy online from a company you know offline to ensure they are trustworthy, or read the reviews (either on news-stand publications or online magazines) of the equipment you need, and then purchase it online. The advantage of most online purchases is the discounts available (this is especially true for office equipment like furniture and stationery), and it is this which will maintain the internet as a strong shopping resource.

Telecoms, despite the downturn in the sector's fortunes in 2001, is an ever-developing industry. The big players in the telecoms business such as BT Cellnet, Orange, and Vodafone are falling over themselves to offer special services to businesses, and all are worth a trawl before making your purchasing decisions. But just when you thought you had the state-of-the-art phone system/mobile, it's obsolete. The TelecomsAdvice site featured here provides a wonderful reference point to keep you up-to-date with new products on the market (and to explain the rather bewildering jargon).

www.biz4less.co.uk
Business Centre

Overall rating: ★ ★ ★ ★			
Classification:	shopping	**Readability:**	★ ★ ★ ★
Updating:	regularly	**Content:**	★ ★ ★ ★
Navigation:	★ ★ ★ ★	**Speed:**	★ ★ ★ ★

UK

Designed for SMEs, the Business Centre section of Biz4Less gives a selection of companies selling business equipment and services, so those in the market can compare and contrast prices. It's partly a portal site, with direct links through to the sites of the recommended suppliers, though the site claims no responsibility for its recommendations. A nice touch is the emphasis on good UK companies as well as the international heavyweights like UPS, Gestetner, and Manpower.

SPECIAL FEATURES

Shopping Area covers your personal shopping needs with items from books to toys and computers, and direct links that include Amazon, Dell and Egg.

Business Centre is located in the index across the top of the and lists a complete run down on items and services for sale. These include office supplies, equipment, and furniture; office services; computers, software and internet services; health and safety equipment; HR services, maintenance supplies; communications and couriers.

Once you have chosen a sector and picked a supplier you like the sound of, its site appears as a pop up menu.

Biz4less has done the donkey work for you in whittling down the number of suppliers in each category to ones worth bothering with.

www.bsa.org.uk
Business Software Alliance

Overall rating: ★ ★ ★			
Classification:	information	**Readability:**	★ ★ ★
Updating:	regularly	**Content:**	★ ★ ★
Navigation:	★ ★ ★	**Speed:**	★ ★ ★ ★

UK US

Not a site you will need to come to often, but useful when in the market for buying software. Since 1988, the Business Software Alliance (BSA) has been 'the voice of the world's leading software developers before governments and with consumers in the international marketplace'. This is the UK version of the global site whose mission statement is to educate computer users on software copyrights and fight software piracy – the site highlights the fact that in the UK one in four software packages used in business are illegal.

To this end the site promotes the software audit return for businesses to check their software legality; there is a UK and world-wide news link, and hints for shopping for software online. The latter is a US feature, but the guidelines for spotting pirated software are just as relevant here.

If you are a new business person with a software product to safeguard, or are simply worried about the legality of the software that you use, then this site is an excellent refernce point.

www.computerbuyer.co.uk
Computer Buyer Magazine

Overall rating: ★ ★ ★ ★			
Classification:	information	**Readability:**	★ ★ ★ ★ ★
Updating:	regularly	**Content:**	★ ★ ★ ★
Navigation:	★ ★ ★ ★	**Speed:**	★ ★ ★

UK   R

The online version of the Dennis Publications news-stand magazine, this site contains all the information in current issues as well as a two year archive. Find the buyer's opinion on hardware and software, and what the experts think. Search for something specific, browse by category. The Helper bar on the left will bring up the best prices for the item you're reading about.

Browsers need to register (a rather long and tedious process that offers access to newsletters from other publications in the group) before access is given to the features and reviews. This doesn't help what is already an incredibly slow loading site – too many flashing icons, which, irritatingly, are adverts for the most part.

SPECIAL FEATURES

Reviews can be searched by product or category. The blue box covers recent reviews, the drop down box is the two year archive, and is huge. The text isn't long but the writing is bright, and to the point.

Top 50 is just that covering PCs (categorised as over and under £850), software, inkjet and laser printers, office software, miscellaneous hardware and other software for home use (i.e. kids). Products are star rated and include the price, the date of the review and a contact number for purchase.

Know-How is excellent with advice and information split as Hints and Tips, and Step by Step, for the computer virgin and the more advanced geek. Find out how to create a mail shot, sort out taxes online, audit your spreadsheet, check out duty and tax to name but a handful. Most are brief with links to relevant sites.

OTHER FEATURES

Guides feature online auctions, with the inevitable link to eBay, advertising for car finance and insurance. There are also links to other titles in the publishing group, a voting page, competition and chat room.

If you can bear to wait until the site loads, there is much here to save time when looking to buy office hardware and software. The information is right up-to-date, and the text chatty and readable.

www.ezoka.com
eZoka

Overall rating: ★ ★ ★ ★			
Classification:	shopping	**Readability:**	★ ★ ★ ★
Updating:	regularly	**Content:**	★ ★ ★ ★
Navigation:	★ ★ ★	**Speed:**	★ ★ ★

UK   R

EZoka claims to provide net purchasing power. The site gets off to a good start as all good websites should, and the homepage kicks off with 'What is eZoka?'. The idea is that from the site SMEs can purchase all their office goods and services through the company, who can negotiate the best terms with global suppliers (it stresses that no damaged or excess inventory goods are included).

Purchasers need to register, with full company details, though registration is free, and can then login in to pages customised to offer goods in their postal area. Do it this way, or search the site for what you want, then register. The site also offers a rebate scheme: the more you spend or recommend the site, the more discount you receive. The site also offers payment options and credit accounts.

SPECIAL FEATURES

Items for sale are broken down into categories, in the index to the left of the page:

They cover:

• Courier services

• Networking, communications and accessories such as cables and keyboards

• Office products and supplies, which contains one item in the former category (fax machines), and furniture and stationery in the latter. Stationery covers everything down to paper clips

• PC e-starter options and accessories with desktops and laptops supplied by Hi-grade Computers

• Printers and office equipment including storage and security

• Telephony covering both mobiles, from all the major names and fixed line phones

• Televisual Products from Toshiba

• Utilities covering gas and electricity suppliers

Find specific items or brands using the Quick Search or go through the product categories mentioned, though beware as the search is refined and refined. The site works on a shopping trolley system, and credit card or other payment details are requested on check out.

OTHER FEATURES

EZoka lists several special offers and promotions on the home page, from discounted products to interest free credit and travel vouchers.

On Demand is an email facility if you cannot find the product you are looking for in the search facility. A response in promised within one working day.

With the About eZoka page there is a list of useful links to SME related sites, including business associations, tax and legal sites, finance, travel (just the Railtrack Timetable here), government sites, search engines and information directories. Run the mouse down the left hand column to bring up related links.

Though some categories are thin, the basis of the site is sound and clearly explained, with money to be saved especially for those buying in bulk.

www.technologymeansbusiness.org.uk

Technology Means Business

Overall rating: ★ ★ ★			
Classification:	information	**Readability:**	★ ★ ★
Updating:	regularly	**Content:**	★ ★ ★
Navigation:	★ ★	**Speed:**	★ ★ ★

UK   R

Another DTI agency, managed by the Institute of Management, this time committed to raising the standard of ICT and business advice to small and medium sized enterprises. 'Business advice needs to take account of the implications and opportunities presented by technology,' it claims, and the site aims to provide news and IT events information, as well as a directory of business and IT advisers by region or speciality.

The site is painfully slow and you might be tempted to throw in the towel before you get started. The information is also badly organised, which means that at times it can be a little unclear. The homepage provides you with little direction, and you will need to go to Benefits or About Us to find out the raison d'etre of it all.

SPECIAL FEATURES

The site is split for advisers and those seeking advice. Business-orientated techies can register to become accredited, though the site also promotes the services of knowledge accredited advisers, which is government jargon for those who are part-qualified. Registration gives advisers access to a 'range of tools/information and resources' for around £150 plus VAT

For businesses that are just starting out or interested in updating their ICT, the adviser search is done by region, postcode or speciality. Search by region and you are given a list of accredited and knowledge accredited people, with an email link, but no mention of their speciality.

OTHER FEATURES

The Business area of the site lists news items and venues for IT events, with a news and press release archive.

Useful Info (there's that feeble drop down menu again) provides links to the sites of the agency's sponsors (BT, Compaq, Intel and Microsoft) as well as a small handful of others such as eZoka and NFEA.

Valuable from the point of view of its directory of advisers (but who are they and what can they do?). Could do better.

www.telecomsadvice.org.uk
Telecoms Advice

Overall rating: ★ ★ ★ ★			
Classification:	information	**Readability:**	★ ★ ★ ★
Updating:	regularly	**Content:**	★ ★ ★ ★ ★
Navigation:	★ ★ ★ ★	**Speed:**	★ ★ ★ ★

UK

Just the sort of website to refer to when you have basic and more detailed questions about telecoms and the internet which need straightforward answers. TelecomsAdvice is independent and set up for small businesses in response to a recommendation by Oftel's Small Business Task Force, to give an overview of the basic information, products and services on offer.

Search the site by keywords, follow the index or go to the excellent site map which is clearly laid out.

SPECIAL FEATURES

Index is split into nine areas, with features, information 'sheets' and in some cases FAQs in each category. Some of the information overlaps, which is forgivable as it makes coverage more thorough.

Buyer's Guide has four features and 19 information sheets, which run from a buyer's guide to mobile phones and the internet, to sources of help for SMEs and getting broadband connectivity. All the features are easy to read (most written by Crucible Multimedia) and no one is going to make you feel a fool for wanting to know about the 'local loop' for example.

Your Web Presence runs from the basics of registering a domain name to web design, and Take Care covers well the legal issues behind web information, 'netiquette' (a great

new word for the 21st Century) and the way to write an email, a comparatively new area of law which is lining the pockets of the libel lawyers.

What's the Technology is the real buffer's page, answering basic 'what is' questions from the internet, to Centrex and DECT phones. From here, there is Working in the Information Age with information on using a mobile abroad etc.

Doing Business Online has a feature on Building a Customer Relationship Strategy, and information on using email, updating mailing lists (amongst others) and an FAQ section, for example: Can we take our fixed line numbers when we move our business? Getting Connected has the basics of setting up an efficient office telecoms system.

In case you need light relief, Just For Fun has a piece on mobile phone tones and graphics.

Background tells you all about Oftel, has a foreword from the chairman and information about the heavyweight sponsors behind the site. Browsers also have the opportunity to subscribe to the newsletter.

Excellent resource of basic information on all areas of landline, mobile phone and internet communications. One gripe: there is no means to return back to the home page, but we're just being picky. This site will suit luddites, those willing to learn and those who need to complete their teccie credentials.

Buying Computers/Hardware Online

Apple
http://Store.apple.com

Dell
www.dell.co.uk

Compaq
www.compaq.co.uk

Evesham Micros
www.evesham.com

Hewlett Packard
http://welcome.hp.com/country/uk

IBM
www.ibm.com

Intel
www.intel.com

Microwarehouse
www.microwarehouse.co.uk

PC World
www.pcworld.co.uk

UK 250
www.computer-websites.co.uk
Portal site for computer purchasing online.

Vitec
www.vitec.co.uk

W Store|
www.wstore.co.uk

Buying Software Online

Some sites advertise their own software systems. Others like PCWorld and DabsDirect are computer supermarkets, selling software split into categories and sub-categories. Search by subject (Small Business Solutions for example) then by type of software: anti-virus, business tools, graphics and design, accounts. In the case of DabsDirect some software can be downloaded immediately.

Barclays Bank Business Park
www.businesspark.barclays.com/shop.htm

Dabs Direct
www.dabs.com

Microsoft
www.microsoft.com

Novatech
www.Novatech.co.uk

Palm
www.palm.com

PC World
www.pcworld.co.uk

SMC Direct
www.smcdirect.com

Software Options
www.software-options.com

WStore
www.wstore.co.uk

Telecoms Sites:

AT&T
www.att.com
US site with Small Business Centre

BT Cellnet
www.btcellnet.net

British Telecom
www.bt.com/sme

Cable & Wireless
www.cw.com
Select SMEs and UK in drop down menu.

Orange
www.orange.co.uk/business

Nokia
www.nokia.co.uk

Vodafone
www.vodafone.co.uk
Click on Business in the index.

Your Communications
www.yourcommunications.co.uk

Chapter 7

government & business organisations

So far the book, on the whole, has looked at independent business-to-business organisations. However, information for small businesses, either direct from the government or through government agencies, is surprisingly good, and with the enormous percentage of all businesses employing less than 50 people, it's an area the government should indeed be actively supporting.

There is more here than governmental encouragement however; there is information about doing business in Europe and it is now even possible to register your new business, change company details and carry out company searches from the comfort of your PC. Amongst the group is BusinessLink which, with its warren-like resources of information, is one of the best business sites on the Internet.

The chapter also looks at those government departments which deal with taxation – an aspect of life it is impossible to ignore – but the power of the internet has even reached here too. Returns can now be filed online, tax information gleaned from Inland Revenue advisors, and information about IR35, the legislation covering freelancers on long term contracts, is well covered.

www.britishchambers.org.uk

The British Chambers of Commerce

Overall rating: ★ ★ ★			
Classification:	organisation	**Readability:**	★ ★ ★ ★
Updating:	monthly	**Content:**	★ ★ ★ ★
Navigation:	★ ★ ★	**Speed:**	★ ★ ★

UK

A mammoth site, cataloguing all that membership of the British Chambers of Commerce (BCC) can offer, plus free access to BCC press releases and survey results. If you weren't already aware, the BCC is a national network of independent, non-profit making organisations whose role is to support local business and to lobby government on small business issues.

The homepage offers something of a mish-mash of items from news releases and topical special features, to invitations to join surveys and the highlights of the site. The index is easier to follow and the site map the best overview of all.

SPECIAL FEATURES

Find Your Chamber is accessible via the drop down menu listing towns, or by clicking on a slow loading UK map. Once you have selected your town or area, there are links to your local BCC website.

News is a well laid-out listing of press releases and survey results (including the influential BCC Quarterly Survey), identifiable by good, clear icons. Subjects covered include economy and tax, small firms and employment issues, Europe and International trade, education and training, company and financial affairs, transport, IT and legal and regional affairs.

Export Zone is a spectacularly good area of the site, aimed at potential and expanding exporters. Items covered with

the same, clear icons include market research and excellent country profiles. Click on the world map under the continent of interest, then on the particular country for a full page feature on the population and economic activity. Each country page includes local advertisers, and the index has useful information including weather, world news and phone codes. Other items covered include useful contacts for further information on organisation and specific markets not covered by the BCC, export procedures, business matchmaking worldwide and a link to Trade Partners UK.

Business Benefits lists the privileges BCC members are entitled to. These are pretty comprehensive with savings on telecoms, fleet management systems, utilities discounts, healthcare policy offers, a translation service and employees counselling service. The stakeholder pensions page has comprehensive information about the whys and wherefores of the new scheme and a link to www.chamberspensions.com, the exclusive BCC online pension buying facility.

OTHER FEATURES

Members and browsers can find information about the BCC 2002 Conference and review of last year's event. The Bookshop offers 10 BCC publications and reports to purchase online. Key Links is excellent, though lists just useful business contacts with no explanations about who or what they are. Partners gives information about BCC partners such as Cisco, Mondus.co.uk and the Royal Mail's online e-commerce facility ViaCode. Here and elsewhere in the site there is access to information about ChamberSign, set up in association with ViaCode, an application form in PDF format.

Good information here from a big player in the small business world. Interestingly there appears to be no information about joining the BCC. Does one go to one's local website first?

www.businessconnect.org.uk

Business Connect Wales

Overall rating: ★ ★ ★ ★			
Classification:	information	**Readability:**	★ ★ ★ ★
Updating:	occasionally	**Content:**	★ ★ ★ ★
Navigation:	★ ★ ★ ★	**Speed:**	★ ★

UK R

Links are very thorough and cover categories such as business services, colleges, Government bodies, IT and design, local authorities and technology.

A useful and comprehensive site for Welsh SMEs for information purposes. Heavy on graphics so suffers from being too slow.

Business Connect Wales is an alliance of agencies (TECs, WDA, Local Authorities, Enterprise Agencies and other local partners) providing publicly-funded business support, and co-ordinates the latest information, advice and assistance available to small and medium sized businesses in Wales. Advice can be found either online or through a low cost phone number (08457 96 97 98).

Without logging on browsers can view local centre locations throughout Wales, case studies, up-coming events and FAQs about BCW. Registering gives access to Barclay's sponsored advice notes on over 200 issues, a schemes and grants directory, links to all the major players in Wales, a Forum for Business and online access to key internet resources for Business. Most of the site is in English, though some information is translated into Welsh by clicking on 'Cymraeg'.

SPECIAL FEATURES

Case Studies consists of reports on people BCW has worked with, and clicking on the Wales map gives addresses of BCW's centres.

What's New provides stop press articles as well as features on such as a legislation watch, with current issues such as new outlines for VAT registration.

www.businesslink.org
Business Link

Overall rating: ★ ★ ★ ★ ★			
Classification:	information	**Readability:**	★ ★ ★ ★ ★
Updating:	regularly	**Content:**	★ ★ ★ ★ ★
Navigation:	★ ★ ★ ★ ★	**Speed:**	★ ★ ★ ★ ★

UK R

If we had stayed on this website any longer, this book would never have been written. Five stars all round for a brilliantly put together body of information. It feels a bit like the Hampton Court Maze, with one avenue leading to another and another…This is all the more laudable when you discover that the site is still under construction and, though some of the links could do with padding out, the bones of the site are there and there's some flesh in evidence too.

The site is provided by the Small Business Service (www.sbs.org.uk), a government agency. SBS was established in April 2000, and works closely with the Parliamentary Under-Secretary of State for Small Business. The site details grants and services SBS can provide such as technology and development grants, and the SBS Small Firms Loan Guarantee Scheme, which guarantees loans from the banks and other financial institutions for small firms that have viable business proposals, but who have tried and failed to get a conventional loan because of a lack of security. The site is easy to follow with a simple index and links within the text, and has a useful section of small business statistics and, rather depressingly, survival rates.

BusinessLink is aimed at those starting a business, as well as those expanding one. Topics covered include starting your business, financing your business, people and places, running your business, technology and innovation, regulations and tax and business opportunities – all laid out in footprints across the screen, before you enter the site. Be prepared for a colossal amount of information (over 500 FAQs and 200 facts sheets and checklists. The Useful Contacts alone come to over 100).

Registration is not essential, and the information and links are there for all to see, but it means that your details are already in the system when you come to request information, and once registered you can keep information in the briefcase to refer back to later. Omit to register and the information is dumped from the briefcase when you log off.

The topics index is explained simply from the start, though the way it works is simple enough to understand, but it's reassuring that Business Link does not assume you are an internet whizz. Once you have chosen a topic – say, starting up – a pull-down menu of options appears covering before starting up, planning and research, finding finance and so on. Within each features, links to further pages are highlighted in bold and at the end of each feature a list of FAQs on that topic appears, which can be viewed, emailed or assigned to your briefcase. The links within the features are distracting, and it's tempting to go off at a tangent before you have finished reading the page. (That's the maze effect for you).

On the right column of each page there is a choice of useful links on the topic you have selected, What's new section, and Business Link Directory.

The beauty of the site is the readability and every subject is dealt with in an accessible way. The site never forgets that, though your business idea may be brilliant, you may not necessarily have a degree from the Harvard Business School.

SPECIAL FEATURES

The Business Link Directory is a listing of the nearest Business Link office in your area and the network of local operators who can offer business support. There are also links to LEDU in Northern Ireland, BISs in highland and SBGs in lowland Scotland, and Business Connect Wales. Search by email or use the phone number provided. You can even email your details for an advisor to contact you.

Jargon Buster is refreshingly honest, and covers: benchmarking jargon, small business terms, e-commerce and IT, property and premises, and social enterprises. A good reference point if you are too embarrassed to ask, and even the simplest acronyms and abbreviations are explained clearly.

Contacts are the weakest link at time of writing, but these will grow as time goes on one suspects. The listings are split between government sites, trade and professionals, and bodies, companies and miscellaneous organisations.

The **Site Map** is excellent, with a flow chart of topics, leading to subtopics and sub-sub topics (these are rather quaintly referred to as The Focus, Siblings and Children).

More Topics is not to be missed, and covers valuable subjects such as social enterprises, selling your business, women in business, and ethnic minorities for example, with relevant links and FAQs.

A top rate site, and one of the easiest to read of the whole genre of small business websites. Another strength is in the design. It utilises the potential of a website to the nth degree. A great starting place, with especially good information for start ups, but just as useful for expanding businesses. Not surprisingly most of the links are to government websites, but sites like ShellLivewire and UK Public Libraries get an airing too. Fills the heart with joy.

www.companieshouse.gov.uk
Companies House

Overall rating: ★ ★ ★			
Classification:	information	Readability:	★★★
Updating:	regular	Content:	★★★★
Navigation:	★★★★	Speed:	★★★

UK

This straightforward site is split into five main sections:

SPECIAL FEATURES

Guidance Booklets and FAQs Within the booklets is information about company formation including how to go about it, Plcs, buying a company off-the-shelf, and registering a company. Information appears in menus and is whittled down to individual and specific information. Limited Liability Partnerships are also well covered and the FAQs are offered in Welsh as well as English. The Document Submission Checklist is well-worth a look, with advice on registration and change of company name as well as a checklist for the completion of accounts and the annual return. This section also details Companies House Seminars and Exhibitions.

The Company Search is live on the mainframe database available Monday to Saturday, 7am until midnight. Basic company details on 1.5 million companies appear after a search by current or previous company names, or company number. The company type (Plc and so on), address and accounting details are given, and only a reference number for the type of business. Searchers need to refer to the Companies Act for a translation of the number. This section also covers disqualified directors (search by surname) , and links to a domain name search on the Nominet UK website. Registered domain names include details of the name and

ISP registered by and under and the date of registration. There is also a link to www.patent.gov.uk, the UK Patent Office.

Forms includes forms online on PDF format, forms by post and the relatively new WebFiling Service whereby companies can register and update their company information online.

Products and Services is the WebFiling and Company search facility, as well as access to a monthly CD rom containing information about company names and dissolved companies. In addition to the basic company search, browsers can purchase accounts and certain other company information by credit card. The requested information is delivered to the individual download area, and details of the unique address sent by email. The information is available in multi page Tiff for 10 days and can be downloaded from there.

What's New covers press releases about Companies House Activities.

The new WebFiling facility, is nothing else, makes this an essential site for business start-up as well as those making changes in their business information. Very well written, it would be hard to go wrong.

www.countryside.gov.uk
The Countryside Agency

Overall rating: ★ ★ ★			
Classification:	information	**Readability:**	★ ★ ★
Updating:	rarely	**Content:**	★ ★ ★ ★
Navigation:	★ ★ ★ ★	**Speed:**	★ ★ ★

UK

The result of a merger between the Countryside Commission and the Rural Development Commission, The Countryside Agency does not have any proactive role to play in promoting or helping rural small business, but is a good resource tool for anyone with a small rural business, or thinking of launching one. Pretty to look at, with scenic views of rolling hillsides (enough to make anyone leave the smoke for a nicer office location), the design includes several drop down menus which are too sensitive and get in the way of site navigation.

SPECIAL FEATURES

Our Work covers Land and Economy, Corporate Research, and information on Rural Communities and Transport.

Reception includes information about surveys carried out by the CA, the National Countryside Access Forum and good links to related sites, especially government ones like the Dept. for the Environment and Dept. of Transport.

Information contains an online publication ordering service (literature includes farming and rural business reports), but the Regional Map is very weak and on such a vast scale that it is of little use to anyone seriously interested in rural issues.

A big fish in a rather meagre selection of sites for rural businesses.

www.dfes.gov.uk/index.htm
Department for Education and Skills

Overall rating: ★ ★ ★

Classification:	portal	**Readability:**	★ ★ ★
Updating:	occasionally	**Content:**	★ ★ ★
Navigation:	★ ★ ★	**Speed:**	★ ★ ★ ★ ★

UK

Much of the site is for educators and those being educated, but as hopefully learning leads to a career, there is a page for employers called the Employers Gateway. It will keep you abreast of goings on in the Department vis à vis employment. More useful however for a good list of links to government sites, like the Small Business Service as well as government initiatives like SkillsBase and New Deal.

Rather irritatingly, the list is run over two columns so you have to scroll to the bottom of the page then back up again to look down the second column. But these minor quibbles aside, it's a useful central gathering of government small business-related sites.

A useful site for businesses keeping an eye on employment trends, or with vacancies to fill.

www.ednet-ni.com
Economic Development Network for Northern Ireland

Overall rating: ★ ★ ★ ★ ★

Classification:	information	**Readability:**	★ ★ ★ ★
Updating:	regular	**Content:**	★ ★ ★ ★ ★
Navigation:	★ ★ ★ ★ ★	**Speed:**	★ ★ ★ ★ ★

UK

A beautifully put together portal website, with simple categories and a wealth of information for all Northern Ireland businesses, which is simple to navigate, many roads leading to www.Ledu-ni.gov.uk, the Small Business Agency for Northern Ireland. There are lessons here for others trying to communicate to small businesses. Less is definitely more.

Split into three clear categories, the site covers Start-up, Growing and Business Information (go to the site map for an at-a-glance list of the goodies on offer), and within each section appears a list of article choices. Government publications and regulations are here in abundance, but there's emphasis too on the thought processes behind starting a business and, for existing businesses, plenty for what the politicians call 'the way forward'.

SPECIAL FEATURES

Start-up efficiently deals with the basic issues (training, financing, premises), but also has links to information on trading standards, research resources on market, products and competitors and, with the government information links, deals with intellectual property and licences, and product development (with a link to the Industrial Research and Technology Unit at www.irtu-ni.gov.uk, the Patent Office and the Technology and Software Incubator Centre at the University of Ulster).

Growing also covers the basics (marketing, training, technology, and product development), but provides a link to the Innovation Relay Centre (set up under the European Commission's Fourth Framework Programme for Research and Technological Development), quality outlines and legal information and the LEDU's Management Information System Grant (MIS). There's an explanation of how an MIS audit is carried out, the outcome of which is an indication of what is needed within the business in terms of hardware and software package solutions.

Business Information is pleasingly meaty, and focuses on particular sectors like clothing, electronics, engineering, food, software and textiles. The resource library, technical information and online company information will be very handy, and the site deals with environment issues from the point of view of government, industry and academia. The news section is surprisingly thin, but resources elsewhere more than made up for this blip.

OTHER FEATURES

New businesses can link to Belfast's First Stop Business Shop and the Business Start Programme. Youngsters under 30 can click through to Shell LiveWire (see p.26) for business advice and support, and students will find links to business studies information at Northern Ireland's Universities; the Budget details are listed in full too as are listings of council areas, information on business in Europe, and how to tender for public sector contracts.

Clear, straight forward and well-planned. A must for Northern Irish entrepreneurs and those with a germ of a business idea.

www.enterpriseinsight.co.uk
Enterprise Insight

Overall rating: ★ ★ ★			
Classification: information		**Readability:**	★★★★
Updating: regular		**Content:**	★★★★
Navigation: ★★★★		**Speed:**	★★★
UK			

The website of the government backed organisation, Enterprise Insight, which is in partnership with the British Chambers of Commerce, Institute of Directors and Confederation of British Industry. The long list of supporting organisations is impressive, and includes Business in the Community, The Prince's Trust, and the National Federation of Enterprise Agencies. The aim is to promote an awareness of enterprise amongst the young, and to help teachers with National Curriculum coursework.

SPECIAL FEATURES

Information about **Initiatives Within Schools,** events and the network of business ambassadors organised by Enterprise Insight. Business people interested in becoming ambassadors can email in their information.

The Teachers' Channel links teachers to Young Enterprise (see p.27) and to the DTI's Enterprise Guide, and gives links to regional coordinators.

The Research Document on the site currently is a 2000 MORI survey of youngsters' opinions of the importance of enterprise (apparently 11 to 15 year olds view journalists and MPs as the least admirable professions!)

Though not strictly a small businesses site, a useful resource for students and budding entrepreneurs and business studies teachers.

www.fpb.co.uk
The Forum of Private Business

Overall rating: ★ ★ ★			
Classification:	information	Readability:	★ ★ ★ ★
Updating:	occasionally	Content:	★ ★ ★ ★
Navigation:	★ ★ ★	Speed:	★ ★ ★ ★
UK R			

The Forum's mission statement is a commitment to influencing the laws and policies that affect private business and to supporting businesses to grow profitably. Though it is ostensibly a membership site , there is some information that can be accessed without logging in. But that's not to say there is much there in the first place. Information is gleaned through referendum and surveys of members, the results of which the FPB uses to lobby various influential bodies. Members can also access publications by the FPB, in association with partners like TUC and Institute of Chartered Accountants.

Members have exclusive access to internet courses through VuBiz, the Virtual Business University, with modules on writing a business plan, working the net, electronic commerce amongst others. New benefits also include links to Pickasupplier.com and e-marketplace.

SPECIAL FEATURES

Document Download covers FPB health and safety audits, articles on bank charges and the FPB's employment manual.

Features also cover employment law, business rates, taxation, red tape, bank services and late payment, and the links page has a rather feeble list which (for no apparent reason) includes Canadian and US independent business organisations.

News offers just one story.

Action Plan outlines details of its publications and past successes (including persuading the Bank of Scotland and Nat West to end repayable on demand overdrafts). The FPB's raison d'etre is its ability to lobby the government, banks, HSE and what is the meat of the site is tucked down at the bottom of the homepage. Blink and you'll miss this essential link.

The Forum of Private Business is hiding its light under a bushel. The site is readable but completely lacking in any feel good factor, and the juicy information is hidden away. Very serious, but one which might be worth a subscription.

www.hmce.gov.uk
Customs & Excise

Overall rating: ★ ★ ★ ★			
Classification: information		**Readability:**	★ ★ ★ ★
Updating: weekly		**Content:**	★ ★ ★ ★
Navigation: ★ ★ ★ ★		**Speed:**	★ ★ ★ ★
UK			

Amongst a raft of good, and in some cases excellent government websites, you stumble across Customs and Excise, which is not a subject that thrills many people. The site is on the dry side, and could take a few hints from the Inland Revenue site in terms of design and user-friendliness. Pages are presented with one sentence or a couple of word links, with no explanation of what they are about, so sometimes it's a bit of a struggle to find the information you are looking for.

The site is split between Information for the public and Information for Business, and there's some light relief in the section entitled History.

SPECIAL FEATURES

History explains how proud HM Customs and Excise is to be the oldest government department. Did you now for example that Geoffrey Chaucer, Robert Burns and Adam Smith (of The Wealth of Nations) were all customs officials? If you are short of things to do, you can look up the history of the Department from Pre-Normans to the last century, and there is a link to the National HMCE Museum in Liverpool.

What's New is an archive on press releases on HMCE activities.

VAT is an overview of the tax, including advice for new businesses and information on registration limits.

Customs includes information on rates of exchange.

Excise gives some startling statistics on government revenues from taxation on alcohol, tobacco and gambling.

Intrastat outlines European trade including exchange rates.

Information covers budget information.

Electronic Vat Return Service (EVR) is the highlight of the site. Returns can be filed on line, after a rather complicated process of registration through the Government Gateway website, with the benefit that you have until 12 midnight the day before it is due to file the return. EVR will also calculate amounts due and offers a £50 one-off payment for first time users.

Not the most user-friendly of the government sites, but absolutely essential if you need information on VAT.

www.inlandrevenue.gov.uk
Inland Revenue

Overall rating: ★ ★ ★ ★			
Classification: information		**Readability:**	★ ★ ★ ★
Updating: daily		**Content:**	★ ★ ★ ★
Navigation: ★ ★ ★ ★		**Speed:**	★ ★ ★ ★
UK			

God bless the Inland Revenue. With the introduction of the lovely Mrs Doyle from Father Ted to encourage us all to fill in our tax returns on time, it seems the IR is on a bit of a charm offensive. The website is no exception with a cheery greeting to welcome you. The charm soon wears off, however, as under the news for the day it informs you of a jail sentence for one woman who fiddled her return.

Much as it pains us we have to admit that the website is very thorough, with as much attention to detail as the tax inspectors will give your return. The left hand index is split into Individuals, Business, Practitioners, Employers, Non-Residents, Charities and access to the site in Welsh. The Individuals section gives clear advice on deadlines for filling in your return, advice on self-assessment, where to find your local tax office, business use of cars, FAQs and information about the brilliant IR helpline (free for simple questions your accountant would charge you for the answers to).

SPECIAL FEATURES

Featured Areas are located to the right of the page. These cover the bones of all tax issues, from self-assessment advice to corporation tax, National Insurance contributions, IR35 (rules concerning taxation of people in long-term freelance contracts which came in within the 1999 Budget). There is also access to publications, rates and allowances statistics and information about the IR.

Internet Service for PAYE and Self-Assessment enables tax payers and their agents to send SA100 tax returns to the Revenue over the internet via the Government Gateway, and to obtain software and online forms. The process was not actually available at time of writing, but forms could be filled in for filing at a later date.

Employers is in a clever diary/planner format, the tabs on the left of the page enabling you to see the important events you need to know each month, and what action to take. The tabs on the right of the planner reveal menus for guidance and advice on specific issues such as payroll for new employers, or answers to questions about NI Contributions, IR35, tax credits or self assessment.

Electronic Business and Electronic Commerce are to be found within the Business section, and give information on existing and forthcoming facilities for sending forms to the IR over the internet, and also cover the Government and the IR's ambitions for e-businesses. There's a guide to the tax consequences of trading over the internet as well as guidelines on capital allowances (the Budget 2000 announced that first year capital allowances at a rate of 100% will be available for investments by small businesses in information and communications technologies between 1 April 2000 and 31 March 2003).

Starting-Up in Business gives essential information on the tax implications and steps that new businesses need to take.

Individuals provides advice on tax issues for the self-employed, and those filimg personal tax returns.

A great example of a Government department using the Internet to provide information, advice and online services. Enough to make accountants redundant.

OTHER SITES OF INTEREST

British Standards Institution
www.bsi-global.com
BSI provides world-class expertise in product testing, CE marking, global trade inspection, environmental management, information security, and provision of technical advice to exporters, and includes a range of training and consultancy services.

Department for Education and Employment: Recruitment
www.dfee.gov.uk/recruit
A sound and simple website with advice on 'filling your skills gap' and improving your recruiting – published as part of the Department of Work and Pensions.

Department of Industry Employment Regulations
www.dti.gov.uk/er/regs.html
No frills here, just lists under subject headings so you can gen up on or check employment legislation. There are guidance documents on time off, maternity and paternity leave, trade unions and Sunday trading and Employment Rights Factsheets as published by the Small Business Service. All documents can be ordered in print.

Employment Service
www.employmentservice.gov.uk
The Employment Service is an executive Agency of the Department for Work and Pensions, and provides the 1000 Jobcentres around the country. The website explains how these work, how advertising a job is free; that Jobcentres can provide disability employment training and Work Trials whereby you can see a potential employee in action at your workplace for up to three weeks free of charge. There is also a special section for employers in the construction industry.

Euro Information
www.euro.gov.uk
The Government site designed to provide information on the Euro and to help firms understand the implications its introduction in Europe at the end of 2001 will have had on their business. A self-analysis questionnaire is provided to help businesses unsure if they will be affected, plus the site offers factsheets, and links to resources of further Euro information.

Trade Partners UK
www.tradepartners.gov.uk
A Government website with free information to help UK firms secure overseas sales and investments, and to attract foreign direct investment. Not laid out with the usual clarity found in many government sites, and the A-Z of the site combines a site index with links to useful websites, but an essential one to bookmark for businesses entering into an International market.

Confederation of British Industry
www.cbi.org.uk
The CBI is the UK's premier independent business organisation, established over 35 years ago to blow the trumpet and oversee the interest of British Business. It is a non-profit making, non-party political organisation funded by the subscriptions paid by its members, but its website is a useful resource for keeping one's eye on trends in business and for keeping abreast of business news. Best used for its Business Services such as downloading business surveys or for purchasing CBI publications (several aimed at SMEs), but these have to be bought by fax or snail mail after printing out the order form from the site. The Business Links are a bit thin, and at times unreliable.

Chapter 08

marketing & pr

There is a saying that doing business without advertising is like winking at a pretty girl in the dark. You know what you're doing, but no one else does. There is little point is running any kind of commercial operation unless you tell other people what you are about.

Ironically, considering they are in the business of communication, we found most of the marketing sites pretty lacklustre. Most are industry organisations which contain directories of advertising or public relations companies, and despite occasional articles about how to appoint an agency, you are left to find your own way. The Royal Mail is an exception. It tries very hard to create a role for itself in the brave new world of ecommerce, and the data on direct mail presents a convincing argument.

But an element of successful marketing is knowing what the competition is up to, and the Dun and the company directory in Bradstreet's site could provide some interesting information for your marketing arsenal.

Perhaps the lack of strong marketing sites is because the Internet itself has been a force for change in marketing, providing a whole new avenue of advertising possibilities. For advice on making the most of your website and effective design, see chapter nine.

www.adassoc.org.uk
The Advertising Association

Overall rating: ★ ★ ★ ★			
Classification:	Information	**Readability:**	★ ★ ★
Updating:	occasionally	**Content:**	★ ★ ★
Navigation:	★ ★ ★ ★	**Speed:**	★ ★ ★

UK

The Advertising Association site is a federation of trade associations representing agencies, advertisers, the media and support organisations in public relations and market research. The site is really a portal, but has useful news on advertising issues and provides a full list of members with links to their sites.

SPECIAL FEATURES

Information Centre lists briefings and publications. Click on Recommended Reading on Advertising and Marketing for Small Businesses for an excellent reading list. The entire Practical Guide to Advertising document is available to view on line – and essential reading it is too. Under Advertising Codes there are links to The Advertising Standards Authority for example, where the codes can be seen in full for all areas of advertising and can be down loaded in a PDF file.

Advertising Agencies Information Source simply lists publications with ad agency details, and the names and addresses of the top ten advertising agencies are also listed, but how disappointing that this is as far as it goes.

Worth looking at for The Practical Guide to Advertising if nothing else. A good starting point for business wanting to promote their product or services, and unsure of the machinations.

www.dnb.com/local_home_uk
Dun and Bradstreet

Overall rating: ★ ★ ★ ★			
Classification:	Information	**Readability:**	★ ★ ★
Updating:	regularly	**Content:**	★ ★ ★ ★
Navigation:	★ ★ ★ ★	**Speed:**	★ ★ ★

UK

Dun and Bradstreet is the world's leading provider of business information, and though it does not strictly fit into this chapter, its service is to help businesses keep abreast of their suppliers and ahead of their competitors. The site also has a good advice section on successful marketing strategies and the D&B Learning Centre for in-house or distance learning marketing courses. Though much of the language is full of serious business jargon, the core of the site is useful for all sizes of business.

SPECIAL FEATURES

Free Business Directory lists information on over 1.8 million UK businesses. Search by company name, product or service, town, county or postcode, and the Ask Alix system will provide the basic company information. Unlike the Companies House directory however, most of the D&B listings include an Identifier, whereby, for a £15 plus VAT charge (payable by credit card), you can buy Confidence or Confidence Plus reports. These include D&B risk rating, financial summary, business comparison to similar businesses, special information such as criminal proceedings and information about the company's bankers.

Insights provides facts and statistics on a featured country with D&B risk analysis and export advice. The Insights page has archive information about previously featured countries. Subscribe too to the free D&B newsletter.

Communities covers in-depth tips and information about ecommerce, credit and marketing amongst others. Within marketing, for example, there are articles to help broaden your customer base (i.e. Harnessing The Power Of Your Customer Information). This in turn leads to the Learning Centre which includes courses on business management and communication (credit and financial analysis are the others). Courses are either in the form of workshops, distance learning or in house training, and the list provided is fairly extensive: team management, effective telephone selling and communications are just a taster.

Data Universal Numbering System explains D&B's unique nine digit identification sequence which is internationally recognised as a global business identifier. It acts as a common classifier or identifier for invoices, requisitions, payments, shipping, customs clearance and other business documentation. A D-U-N-S number can be applied for online.

Dun & Bradstreet works with the big league companies, but has much to offer SMEs too. It would benefit from loosening up some of the language.

www.ipa.co.uk
Institute of Practitioners of Advertising

Overall rating: ★ ★ ★			
Classification:	Information	Readability:	★ ★ ★
Updating:	regularly	Content:	★ ★ ★ ★
Navigation:	★ ★ ★	Speed:	★ ★

UK   R

A bit more flashing icons and 'blimp' sounds here than in many sites, so the IPA site is slow to load. This would be acceptable if the information was made easier to follow. As it stands, the search facility of the site is useless unless you know what you are looking for. A site map would be more effective.

The IPA is the industry body and professional institute for what it calls 'the UK's thriving and highly potent advertising and marketing communications business'. All browsers have to register and are given guest status, though certain areas of the site (such as the discussion forum or services section) are available to IPA members only. Guests in certain professions (choose from a drop down menu) will eventually be granted member status. Once you are registered, a pop up box offers you the opportunity to install Bitstream WebFont Player.

SPECIAL FEATURES

Membership provides an IPA Agency search. Search by region, town or agency name, area on the map or specialisation. A % symbol placed in the town or agency box will retrieve a complete listing of members. There is advice here on Choosing An Agency, with links to very thorough documents on selecting a communication agency and an ISBA/IPA/DMA (direct marketing) pitch guide full of useful what-to-do advice.

Resource Centre covers the bare bones of advertising: how it works, codes of practice, FAQs and, curiously a page of quotes, of which there are only two and not very thrilling at that. Statistics gives an industry overview which could prove useful if you are investigating a particular sector, and includes Scottish Advertising information and outdoor and cinema statistics.

Someone has really gone to town on the Links page. It is probably the biggest of any we have seen yet. Once again a % symbol placed in the search box reveals the whole shooting match – which includes archives, publications, news sites, research sites, foreign advertising information, travel info and, for not particular reason, Downing Street! Publications, too, offers a mammoth list of advertising related material, available to be purchased online.

The only place to start if you are looking to brief an advertising agency, whether above the line or direct sales and marketing. Not as user friendly as one might expect from the representative body of the effective communications business.

www.royalmail.com
Royal Mail

Overall rating: ★ ★ ★ ★			
Classification:	Information	**Readability:**	★ ★ ★
Updating:	occasionally	**Content:**	★ ★ ★ ★
Navigation:	★ ★ ★ ★	**Speed:**	★ ★ ★

UK

A veritable colossus of a site, so don't be fooled by the comparatively simple homepage. The presentation is excellent, with lots of pretty graphics and weird and wonderful tricks, though we're curious as to why some pages (notably the homepage) aren't optimised to fit the screen.

Much of the information is for public consumption, but there is plenty for small businesses to investigate – and that word is used advisedly. Each section of the index, provides a sub index, which in turn provides a sub-sub index. So you click on the little words 'Business Advice' and open a Pandora's Box. The wisdom of this is debatable. Browsers can find themselves lost – you begin to question whether you have already referred to a page, and where was it you started anyway?

The raison d'etre of the business details within the whole site is to encourage companies to use direct mail as a forerunner and promotion for their advertising (especially e-commerce).

SPECIAL FEATURES

2nd Internet Age gives an overview of 'e-strategy issues facing business today' or how to attract people to your website. The section, in a round about way with plenty of advice and analysis thrown in, invites browsers to register for a free E-Strategy Resource Pack with articles from the

Henley Centre and the Harvard Business School. Within the sales pitch comes some interesting information on Media Options and Brand Awareness; that people prefer to buy brand goods on line from companies they have dealt with off-line (ergo, use direct mail as part of your advertising budget). There are case studies on NetBenefits and Persil to ponder, and some good links which include www.emarketer.com, a provider of internet statistics and www.dmis.co.uk, for information on direct mail.

Not surprisingly the site majors in on the benefits on Clear Addressing, and provides information and advice on envelope design, machine readable mail, barcoded mail and pre-printed postage.

Customer Relationship Management (CRM) occupies an enormous chunk of space, with in depth analysis of current practices in CRM and how few companies are using it. The features continues for page after page, finishing with an Action Plan and a case study from Xerox and Boots, but the relevance to Royal Mail is not obvious, until you turn to...

Data Management which details how Royal Mail can assist with managing address data. There's a link to MailMax, interactive software to estimate how much money companies waste on inaccurately addressed mailings. There are tips on managing a database, and products and services Royal Mail can provide, including CD rom database with Address Finder and Address Manager, PAF (Postcode Address File) database and postcode reference book. The Shop has facilities to purchase stamps and envelopes for business online.

E-Commerce covers similar territory as 2nd Internet Age, with information on achieving successful websites, and tips on CRM, logistics and branding, with a PDF download facility for all the information.

Going Global is a bit weak, with fairly brief country briefings (perhaps it was meant literally?) covering Europe, the US, Finland, Japan and New Zealand. This diverse choice is not explained. Browsers can order a free copy of International Postal Services for Business. Oversees Business deals with travel information, by clicking on the world map and selecting the particular country. Passport and Visa information, money, health, business profiles, history and government, amongst others are very general, but not surprising as it's a hefty database of countries to cover.

Your Business Mail addresses the issues concerning small businesses, with links to other areas of the site covering postal services, marketing advice (see above) and 'further advice', which covers franking machine standards and packing.

Four stars for effort and for looking pretty in a raft of fairly run-of-the-mill sites. But one can't help feeling the good old Royal Mail has over-stretched itself, probably in response to the electronic mail revolution. The site would benefit from simplification; fewer pages, with their eye kept firmly on the point it is trying to make.

See also www.uk-po.co.uk, the Consignia Site .

OTHER SITES OF INTEREST

British Market Research Association

www.brma.org.uk/selectline and www.brma.org.uk

Registration site for listings of BRMA Members, organised by geographical region, alphabetically or by specialism. Main site has listings alphabetically but no indication of details about the companies. This site does however have a feature on choosing a market research company.

Commercial Radio Companies Association

www.crca.co.uk

The trade body for commercial radio companies, so much of the site is for members usage, but worth looking at when considering which stations to place your radio advertising. To select from the CRCA Members List, choose from the drop down menu which is split into FM and AM stations, digital and by company name. Listings include contact details, email and website link. To access audience figures, there is a direct link to www.rajar.co.uk (Radio Joint Audience Research Ltd). Once in this site go to Quarterly Summary for a complete chart of audience figures for almost all commercial radio stations. There is also a link within the site to the Radio Advertising Clearance Centre.

Direct Marketing Association

www.dma.org.uk

The DMA (UK) Ltd is the trade organisation for companies in direct marketing in the UK, and though half of the site is for member access only, there is information open to all. Areas of interest to businesses investigating direct marketing would be the Members Directory search. This is managed by name or place, or by services offered of which there is a broad choice. Industry Standards outlines the DMA code of practice, and specialist areas such as communicating to children online. The DMA How-to Guides sound just the ticket, but sadly would not load for us despite several attempts. Perhaps you will have better luck. Useful for accessing direct marketing companies, but not much else.

Millward Brown Market Research

www.millwardbrown.com

The US site seems to cover all MB business. Choose from a selection of marketing queries such as 'Has my marketing plan worked?', 'How strong is my brand?', and you are taken to details of the Millward Brown product designed to find the answers.

Mintel

www.mintel.com

Main site of the big market research company. By registering browsers have the facility to buy Mintel reports and view them instantly online. There is also access to reports catalogue and contents pages free of charge.

Interactive Advertising

www.iabuk.net

This site has plenty for businesses investigating internet advertising as a marketing vehicle. The IAB is growing in importance as a trade association for the young internet advertising industry, and much of the content (though well hidden) provides a valuable resource. Archives features research into the effectiveness of internet advertising and Website traffic figures provide figures for 144 major sites. The IBA stresses figures are for page traffic not reach or frequency. There are also Case Studies of major internet ad campaigns and competitions, in addition to comprehensive company listings and FAQs.

Public Relations Consultants Association

www.martex.co.uk/prca

The website to refer to if you haven't used a PR agency before, or if you are looking for one with a particular speciality. The PRCA site is the federation for public relations consultants, so much of the information is aimed at them. However certain areas such as PR View (which provides listings of 130 UK-based PR consultants) are useful for small businesses as a starting point.

Chapter 09

putting your company online

Having a presence on the web can be a great boost to your business. It can also be a great drain on your resources, if the time and effort you put into your website outstrip the revenue that you gain from it. For many small businesses a company website could be viewed as another marketing tool to complement your print marketing campaign. For some, this may mean a single page providing contact details and a few details about the company to let the potential customer/client know that you are bona fide.

For others, it might mean a more complex site with facilities such as an online ordering system, so that once your clients have found you, they can strike while the iron is hot, and you can instantly gain another customer.

Remember though, that the services offered in cyberspace have to be backed up in the real world, which means time and expense that may well need be diverted from a workforce that is already working to capacity. You'll need to think carefully about how you are you are going to fund and maintain a website.

Getting a website right also requires a number of elements to come together to present a professional image. This chapter will show you how.

getting online

Hardware

There are many brands of personal computer, generally identified by their Operating System. Most are IBM compatible PCs, which run on the Microsoft OS (Windows) although some IT professionals prefer LINUX. Apple Macintosh computers make up the remainder, running on their own Mac OS. Whilst all can be connected to the internet with relative ease, some software will only run on a particular system, although much is available in a range of formats (MS Office, for example, is available in a Mac version). To a great extent it is a matter of personal taste, and requirements. Media and design companies tend to use Macs, but PCs predominate in most industries. Whilst Macs are generally seen as more user-friendly, with an intuitive look and feel, there is an undeniably greater range of software available for PCs. If problems of compatibility with key suppliers and freelancers are to be avoided, some forethought may be required.

Connection

Modems are devices which convert data into an analogue format, so that it may be transmitted via a phone line, and whilst most new computers will have an internal modem, older, more basic models may require an external modem. The current standard is 56kbps so there is little to be gained by buying a modem which is incapable of reaching this speed, although you will seldom find that your connection actually runs that fast, unless you have an ISDN, ASDL or other broadband.

Internet Service Provider (ISP)

If you think of the internet as a series of islands, and your computer as one of these islands, your ISP would be the ferry operator that ensures that data travels between islands. An ISP takes care of the technical side of your connection to the internet, providing access to email, newsgroups and the world wide web through a dial-up account. There are a wide variety of ISPs available and, as ever, the best service is dependent on what you require. See Choosing an ISP below for more details.

Browsers

These are software packages that provide you with a desktop interface through which to navigate the world wide web. Most computers come with a browser already installed, with MS Internet Explorer and Netscape Navigator being the most common. Browsers can also be obtained, free of charge, either from your ISP or from free CD roms available with many internet magazines. To upgrade your browser, or to download an alternative, try www.netscape.co.uk or www.ie.com/downloads.

Email Accounts

These days it is essential to have email access. Most ISPs will provide you with an email address, although j.bloggs90210@yourlocalsupermarket.co.uk may not be the corporate identity you had in mind. Another, relatively inexpensive option is to purchase a domain name (a simple .co.uk registration can cost as little as £10) and you can set up your account to redirect your mail to your ISP account. Don't forget to configure your email software (such as MS Outlook, Eudora) so that it reflects the name of your company.

Virus Protection

A word of warning: since your connection to the internet allows a two-way transfer of data, care must be exercised in order to prevent your computer from 'contracting' any viruses. Viruses are, essentially, nuisance programs that can enter your system via websites, emails (particularly attachments) or hidden in downloads of various kinds. The level of nuisance they represent can range from the merely annoying (such as posting rude messages on your desktop) to the destructive (such as erasing or reformatting your hard drive). It is therefore advisable to install anti-virus software,

such as Norton Anti-Virus or McAfee, and ensure that you scan all downloads and attachments for viruses before they can attack your system.
See:

www.macafee.com
www.symantec.com (for Norton)
www.drsolomon.com

For comparisons of anti-virus software see:
www.cnet.com/software/

Firewalls

If the data on your system is sufficiently valuable, or vulnerable, it may be worth investigating the installation of a Firewall. This effectively restricts traffic in and out of your system, which should prevent unauthorised access to your network. There are a variety of approaches available, involving hardware, others software, but it is advisable to seek advice on the subject.

choosing an ISP

Free ISPs

Nothing in life is free, and while you don't have to pay any subscription charges to use free ISPs, you will have to pay the cost of the 'call'. This is generally an 0845 number, or equivalent, charged at the standard BT rate for a local telephone call. However the Technical Support lines can be expensive, often charging between 50p and £1 per minute. On the whole free ISPs are of best value to an occasional user, who connects to the internet for perhaps four hours, or less, per week. Examples include the following.

Connect Free	www.connectfree.co.uk
Supanet	www.supanet.com
Freeserve	www.freeserve.com

MSN Free Web	www.msn.co.uk/specials/freeweb
Virgin Net	www.virginnet.com
UK Online	www.ukonline.co.uk
Waitrose	www.waitrose.com/free_isp/index.asp
Total Serve	www.totalserve.co.uk

Unmetered ISPs

Instead of costly phone calls, these ISPs provide a freephone 0800 access number, and charge you a monthly subscription fee (from £8.99) for 'unlimited' access to the internet 24 hours a day, 7 days a week or during off-peak periods. This does not mean that you can have a constant internet connection. Most companies have an Acceptable Usage Policy that states how long you are allowed to stay connected before you are automatically cut off. This is usually after 2-4 hours, and is designed to ensure that others are able to connect. Be cautious about cheaper, over-subscribed ISPs, since it may be more difficult to connect at peak times (i.e. 6pm-10pm)

Mad As A Fish	www.madasafish.com
BT Internet	www.btopenworld.com/login_new
AOL	www.aol.co.uk
Clara Net	www.clara.net
Free Chariot	www.freechariot.co.uk
Free Online	www.free-online.co.uk
Vispa	www.vispa.co.uk
Tiscali	www.tiscali.co.uk
Surf Anytime	www.surfanytime.co.uk
IC24	www.IC24.com

Broadband ISPs

Broadband is a relatively new method of connecting to the internet, which allows high-speed access. The data is transferred digitally, over optic-fibre cable, rather than an analogue signal over a phone line. While costs have dropped significantly, it remains more expensive than telephone ISPs and is still not available everywhere. Connection costs start at about £25 mark, with monthly fees of around £20.

Home Choice	www.homechoice.co.uk
NTL	www.askntl.com/locales/gb/en
BT Broadband	www.btopenworld.com/broadband
Blue Yonder	www.blueyonder.co.uk/info

For further information on UK ISPs, log-on to an ISP comparison site, such as www.net4nowt.com.

First work out your objectives. It is important to be clear about these: do you want a simple web-presence to let the

setting up your own website

world know where you are and what you do, or would it be useful to have an online catalogue and the ability to sell your product online? Whichever route you choose, you need to consider how and how often the site will need to be updated – nothing looks sadder than a website that obviously hasn't been touched for six months or longer. If you are likely to need to make changes to the site regularly, you will need to make sure either that you will have the ongoing budget to pay a third-party consultant to do it for you (this can be an expensive option) or roll up your sleeves and learn the basics yourself (or delegate to a more technically minded colleague!).

Web Editing Software
You should discuss with whomever is responsible for creating your site (if you aren't going to do it yourself) what will be required in terms of maintainance, so that you will know which web-authoring tools you will need, and can arrange for some training. Once you get the hang of the programme, almost any computer-literate person should find this possible.

Web pages are usually constructed in HTML (Hyper Text Mark-up Language). The basics are easily self taught from a book or tutorial.

For some idea of what's required, you might try one of these sites, or try entering 'HTML Tutorial' in a search engine (such as Google).

www.davesite.com/webstation/html
www.htmlgoodies.com/primers/basics/html

However, if your pages are going to be anything more than plain text, hand coding is a laborious task, and for more complex projects, a text-editing programme will prove invaluable. At a basic level Microsoft Office programmes allow you to save pages as HTML but generally you will get better results from one of the following

Microsoft FrontPage2000 – not available for Macs and not a favourite with professional designers, but its interface is very familiar to users of Microsoft Office applications.

Macromedia Dreamweaver – expensive but recommended as being easy to use yet giving professional results.

Adobe GoLive – integrates well with other Adobe products such as photoshop.

Handling Images
Adobe Photoshop is the industry standard for image editing, but there are many cheaper packages, some of which are supplied in cut-down editions when you buy a scanner. You need an image editor to resize any images, logos or photos that you want to use on your site. It is important that they are saved at a fairly low resolution (certainly not photo quality) or your web pages will be very slow to load.

choosing a web host

Look in any internet magazine and you'll be confronted with a bewildering array of offers for hosting your website, some that look too good to be true, and they often are. But the real price of web space (which is little more than just storage on a computer without a terminal) need not be high. To compare what's on offer you need to look at all the variables.

Price

This can vary from free to thousands of pounds per year. Consider carefully what your needs really are and don't let a consultant talk you into a Rolls Royce when you could happily get away on a little scooter. Don't forget that ordinary customers can't see where your server is housed, so unless you are very obviously using a free service, complete with their logo and adverts, only pay for what you need.

Email accounts

If the number you can set up is limited, consider just what your needs are likely to be. In an expanding business you might want a separate email address for each member of staff plus general ones such as info@yourcompany or sales@yourcompany.

Webspace

The deals vary from 5MB to unlimited webspace. The former is adequate for about 8-10 fairly simple pages, so if you've got a very complex site, with lots of graphics or a large database, make sure the hosting plan you're using will leave you room to expand and leave enough webspace for backups and email if you're running it from the same server.

Bandwidth

It is difficult to calculate the amount of bandwidth you will need as it is a factor of the size of the pages or documents downloaded from your site, and the amount of traffic visiting the site. Realistically most small businesses and freelancers will be lucky to have the problem of too much traffic, but the extra charges imposed for exceeding your allocated monthly bandwidth can be quite stringent. So if you're planning a red-hot viral marketing campaign that will have tens of thousands of people flocking to your site, it might be worth checking your bandwidth allowance in advance.

Connectivity

The bigger and more expensive the web-hosting service, the more likely it is to have higher level access to the main backbones of the internet (think of it as their own sliproad to a motorway as opposed to a dirt track leading to a B road leading to an A road that connects to the internet). This can affect the speed at which pages from your site download to the viewer's browser and also may effect the availability of your site to viewers. You need to make a judgement about how many of your potential clients will be using broadband connections. If the majority are using 56k modems, they won't really notice the difference.

Server Speed

Just as upgrading your desktop computer to a faster processor can speed up your work, a faster server can theoretically improve your download time. Whether this is perceptible to the majority of users is debatable.

Flexibility

Can you upgrade to a more powerful server easily if you need to, or will you be locked into a fixed-term contract?

Preloaded Software

Does the server support options such as PHP, ASP and MySQL? Check with the person who is building your site what you need, to be pre-installed on your server.

Reliability

Does the company give any guarantees about 'down time', when your site wouldn't be available? Would it matter if your site were down for eight hours?

Security

If your site is mission critical to your business, you may feel reassured if your server is housed in a climate-controlled bunker built to withstand a nuclear blast, with its own firewall, rather than in the back bedroom of a one-man band. But as with most things, you get what you pay for.

Technical Support

The quality varies considerably. Will there be someone at the end of a phone line or email to sort things out promptly, and will you be charged for it? Again rates vary from free to £1 per minute, so if you think you're going to need a lot of help, factor this against any low monthly hosting charges. Check whether the price includes automatic backups of the site. Also find out if support is offered 24-7. Does it matter if your site goes down on a Sunday morning?

Shared/Dedicated Servers

Sharing a server is a cheaper option, and unless you've got a huge site or need to be able to customise your server, sharing will not affect the performance of your site. No one will be able to detect whether your server is shared.

Because it isn't a case of one-size-fits-all, it's hard to recommend individual hosting services, but these sites compare some of the best deals:

www.webhostmagazine.com/index.asp
www.hostcompare.com
www.comparewebhosts.com
www.hostindex.com
www.FindYourHosting.com

payment system options

If you wish to sell goods or services online you will need to set up a secure payment and authorisation system to take credit cards. For most small businesses it is worth using a third-party service for this, unless you will be generating very large volumes of online sales.

Of course, you don't have to offer the option of online payment at all: your site could encourage people to call you, and research suggests that the majority of people still prefer to give credit card details over the phone rather than over the internet. Never ask your customers to email their credit card details to you, as emails can be easily intercepted.

Some of the major high-street banks offer online credit-card payment systems as an extension of their credit-card merchant services, and so if you are already an established merchant they may be willing to extend their online facility to you. They are particularly resistant to internet start-ups and may require large personal guarantees against fraud. You may therefore find a more sympathetic ear from companies such as the ones listed below, who offer payment systems for a small percentage commission on each transaction. Some also offer ecommerce 'shopping basket' packages, which are easy to customise and integrate with your site. Most will remit the money they collect on your behalf directly to your bank account.

As well as comparing commission rates, set-up and service charges, you should consider how long they will hold your money before passing it on to you, as this can have significant implications for your cash-flow.

www.worldpay.com – a popular choice for small businesses offering online sales.
www.netbanx.com
www.datacash.co.uk

marketing a website

You've invested time and money getting a web presence. How do you let people know it's there? Obviously make sure your URL (web address) appears on all your notepaper, business cards, advertisements and promotional materials. Send an email announcing the launch of your site to all of your clients encouraging them to take a look (but not until it is up and running and fully tested) .

Competitions are a good incentive for people to log on to your site. But how do you attract new customers or potential customers to your site?

A 'viral marketing' campaign can be very effective if you can devise the right idea. The object is to provide something on your site that is so clever, funny or useful that when you email someone to tell them about it, they feel it is worth forwarding your email to many of their contacts, who may then forward it to their contacts, driving a wider range of people to your site.

Make sure your URL is submitted to the websites of other relevant companies or organisations: chambers of commerce, trade organisations, clients. Links to your site from other people's sites are one of the best ways of finding new clients. If you have a page of links on your site you can offer to set up reciprocal links with clients, suppliers and other related companies.

Online Advertising

Banner ads require you to commission or create the artwork, and they have a limited response rate unless extremely well-targeted. They are also regarded by many internet users as intrusive. Rather than paying for thousands of random 'page impressions', where you have little or no control over where they appear or whom they are seen by, you may be better off to make a direct approach to the sites you want to appear on.

Search Engine Submission

Most people find new sites on the internet by using a search engine, and therefore your rankings (how close to the top of the list your site appears on searches for particular keywords) can be very important if you want the web to bring you new business. You can either submit your site to the major search engines and directories manually, or use a search-engine submission programme, or a submission service. Although there are hundreds of search engines, there are only a few that really count, and as each engine has very different submission rules, it is most effective to concentrate your efforts on getting the big ones right.

The following sites offer resepected software and/or useful advice about ensuring effective submissions:

www.cyberspacehq.com
http://1stplaceranking.com/resources.htm
www.searchengineguide.com
www.websearchworkshop.co.uk/workbench.htm
www.gmarketing.com

Directories

Many people don't differentiate between search engines and directories, because to the end user the results are much the same: you type your keywords in a search box, and you receive a list of relevant sites. The difference lies in the ways they are compiled: sites in directories are evaluated and classified by humans; search engines send out web-bots, spiders or webcrawlers that automatically trawl through sites and index them according to their particular criteria. Each search engine and directory has its own evaluative criteria, which is why they will give different results. Some also give weight to paid entries, and others share the same underlying technologies. The main search engines and directories are as follows:

Altavista	http://uk.altavista.com
Excite	www.excite.co.uk
Google	www.google.co.uk
Hotbot	www.hotbot.lycos.co.uk
Looksmart	www.looksmart.co.uk
Lycos	www.lycos.co.uk
MSN	www.msn.co.uk
Yahoo	http://uk.yahoo.com

improving your rankings

- Make sure your site is attractive, easy to use and read – some of them are evaluated by people rather than 'webcrawlers' (automatic page indexers)

- Spend time thinking about the keywords and phrases to be used in your page title, headlines and the top of text pages, as well as those embedded in the meta tags in your HTML coding.

- In particular, think laterally about the sorts of words likely to be searched for by the people who would benefit from your goods and services, and which will differentiate you from the competition.

- Don't over-submit your site – some search engines and directories will penalise you if you submit the site too often, without substantial changes to the content.

- Make sure you understand how each search engines and directory works and what their submission criteria are.

- Remember it can take up to three or four months for your site to be indexed or evaluated, although sometimes you can pay for this to be done faster.

- Some search engines award higher rankings to sites that have lots of links to them, particularly if those sites are themselves high ranking. So work on persuading others to link to your site.

- Examine the sites that get higher rankings than yours on competing keywords. Why is their site more successful?

- Make sure your keywords are spelt correctly.

- Add common variations of spellings and misspellings.

- Monitor your rankings and change your keywords frequently

- Register for the Market Position Newsletter at: http://www.marketposition.com

Chapter 10

business travel

Despite exhaustive research, we have been unable to bring you conclusive figures on the amount of money it costs British business to have its executives sitting in traffic jams, airport departure lounges or train station platforms. Perhaps no one can bear to reveal what must be a figure running into tens of millions of pounds.

What can you do to avoid delays? They come with the territory, and as more and more business is carried out around the country, throughout Europe and world-wide, delays will get worse and the costs will escalate. The websites in this chapter provide the best means to find out where the traffic hold-ups are, flight changes or rail cancellations, and as technology advances the information can now be emailed to your PC, text-messaged to your phone, or information accessed via a WAP phone. It is interesting to compare the costs of these services between the various suppliers.

Business travel advice, including country profiles, appear to be excellent. Details about suitable hotels, their facilities and price ranges are only a click away, and with the opportunity to book tickets, hire cars, book airport car parking spaces, arrange currency and accommodation online, and even have visas delivered to your door – business travel arrangements have never been easier. But with the growing use of video conferencing and webcam, one wonders if we can dispense with travel completely?

road travel

www.theaa.com/travelwatch		
AA Travelwatch		
Overall rating: ★ ★ ★ ★		
Classification: Information	**Readability:**	★ ★ ★
Updating: hourly	**Content:**	★ ★ ★ ★
Navigation: ★ ★ ★	**Speed:**	★ ★ ★
UK R		

Bearing in mind the amount of expensive business time wasted sitting in traffic queues, this site is worth bookmarking. The information is thorough and up-to-the-minute, but on the downside it is very slow to load and the jam may have cleared by the time you retrieve the information.

SPECIAL FEATURES

Email Alerts Register to use this service, and give details on your trip, and Travelwatch will email personalised traffic reports. There is also a WAP phone user link for directions and travel news.

Route Planner covers the UK, Ireland and Europe. With the interactive map, you can be very specific about your starting and finishing point, and within a few seconds a detailed route plan will appear. There is also a print out option.

Travel News includes a menu of the latest alerts, or you can search by city or town, or motorway. Click on the area of the motorway map, and alert icons appear with information about the nature of the hold up.

Despite the speed of this site, this is one any business whatever the size should have bookmarked.

www.avis.co.uk		
Avis Car Rental		
Overall rating: ★ ★ ★		
Classification: Information	**Readability:**	★ ★ ★ ★
Updating: occasionally	**Content:**	★ ★ ★
Navigation: ★ ★ ★	**Speed:**	★ ★ ★ ★
UK		

Deep in the depths of the site lies the Avis Advance service. To find it, go to Services and Clubs, then Avis Advance in the index. This outlines the special SME programme offering free membership if your company rents a car at least five times a year. The programme includes cheap rental, use of Avis Preferred (a quick service option) and everyday that you rent you earn a point, and after 15 points you earn a free day.

There is information about the dedicated customer phone line or booking can be made online. Companies are given an Avis Worldwide Discount number to use to obtain points. Joining is not as simple as the site reckons – it involves clicking on the word icon Save Target As ... to download, or double clicking to apply online. The main site offers a quote search and online booking.

OTHER FEATURES

Special Offers outlines weekend booking deals, 7-day booking deals and weekend upgrades.

Guide to Renting details how to go about the process, returning your car, rental locations and insurance.

Online Assistant is a database of answers to questions about Avis service and special programmes.

Not as straight forward as Hertz's site, but essential to look at both to compare the deals.

www.hertz.co.uk
Hertz Car Rental

Overall rating: ★ ★ ★ ★			
Classification:	Information	Readability:	★ ★ ★ ★
Updating:	occasionally	Content:	★ ★ ★ ★
Navigation:	★ ★ ★ ★	Speed:	★ ★ ★ ★

UK

The main Hertz site has a special section for SMEs, outlining the Hertz Business Account Programme, which offers companies that do not have a negotiated contract with the company special car rental rates and benefits.

Called Hertz Link Loyalty, like Avis, it's a points-for-use scheme: receive 10 points for every day's UK car hire. As soon as you get to 120 points, you get a free class C car for one day. Quicker than its rival, the site is wonderfully easy to follow, and SMEs can enrol into the scheme online.

OTHER FEATURES

Rates and Reservations allows online booking, by filling in the boxes with details of where and when you need the car world-wide. Click on the world map for Hertz office locations and special services available, including long term rental and rail and drive schemes.

Products and Services supplies information on weekend special offers, discounts for Virgin Flying Club Members and BA Executive Club Members, and USA offers available only on the internet.

Simple and straightforward site, which reflects the professional, high standards of the company.

www.racbusiness.co.uk
The RAC

Overall rating: ★ ★ ★			
Classification:	Information	Readability:	★ ★ ★
Updating:	hourly	Content:	★ ★
Navigation:	★ ★ ★	Speed:	★ ★ ★

UK

The RAC has the same idea as the AA; route planning, traffic information and hotel booking, and this can be found at the main site at www.rac.co.uk and here on their business site. With information on company fleet assistance for cars and commercial vehicles, insurance and a network of RAC consultants, however, it has stolen a march on its rival. There is also a link to the RAC signs site for information on signposting business events.

SPECIAL FEATURES

Check traffic is a free service to all, with the facility to check by area and sorted by severity, road name or county. It is European wide and can be updated at the click of a button, and the particular roadworks viewed. There is also an offer of a one month free trail on the £35 a year Route Minder (not to be confused with the Route Planner). This gives personalised traffic information with a Live Traffic News Map (with traffic flow information and RAC incident information) and a delay forecast for any journey in the UK.

Route Planner is also open to all, and the search is by town city name, or postcode. The instructions for use are long and complicated. The search is very slow and we failed to get a response to our simple hypothetical route query.

Not as simple as the AA site, and even slower to achieve results, but gains points for its business facilities.

rail travel

www.thetrainline.com

The Trainline

Overall rating: ★ ★ ★			
Classification:	Information	Readability:	★ ★ ★ ★ ★
Updating:	occasionally	Content:	★ ★ ★ ★
Navigation:	★ ★ ★ ★ ★	Speed:	★ ★ ★ ★

UK R

This is the site for the UK rail traveller but when accessing it do not forget the prefix 'the', otherwise you will find yourself looking at the promotional site of a rock band. The Trainline gives details of all train times, ticket bookings and seat reservations on trains in mainland UK.

Registration is required for the first-time user. The site, once you have registered, is easy to use – although the search facility could be faster.

SPECIAL FEATURES

Rail News links through to National Rail's site giving news of disruptions on the lines.

The service is useful for long-term journey planning. Remember to bear in mind delivery time of tickets. For best fares, it may be advantageous to visit the sites of individual rail companies.

www.eurostar.com

Eurostar

Overall rating: ★ ★ ★ ★			
Classification:	Information	Readability:	★ ★ ★ ★
Updating:	occasionally	Content:	★ ★ ★ ★
Navigation:	★ ★ ★ ★	Speed:	★ ★ ★ ★

UK R

Eurostar is a slick operation, with the website especially geared towards its business customers. The Destinations link in the index outlines all eight possible stops, from London, Ashford, Calais, to Paris, Disneyland, and the Alps, and entices you with descriptions of further destinations including Amsterdam, Bordeaux, Bruges, the Loire and Lyon in case your business takes you there.

SPECIAL FEATURES

Timetable works by selecting the day (Mon to Sat, Sunday) and route, and gives a quick response, and you can book online by choosing your destination and you are then linked to the local Eurostar Distributor site. There are no discounts for booking online.

Services and Facilities outlines the benefits to business travellers. These include business lounges, group bookings for meetings, and free papers. Frequent business travellers using the service can register and earn points, which can be exchanged for free train travel, or for use with Eurostar Partners such as American Express. Earn enough and you move from Blue Member through Silver to Gold and the privileges increase.

A swift and responsive site, which manages to reflect the upmarket image of the service without resorting to slow loading graphics.

air travel

http://www.oag.com
OAG Air Business Travel Information

Overall rating: ★ ★ ★ ★

Classification:	Information	**Readability:**	★ ★ ★ ★
Updating:	regularly	**Content:**	★ ★ ★ ★
Navigation:	★ ★ ★ ★	**Speed:**	★ ★ ★ ★

US   R

A superb and helpful site, especially for frequent businesses travellers, and most useful to those with all the state-of-the-art technology to receive information to internet enabled mobile phones or PDAs. OAG, which also publishes its Pocket Flight Guides, claims to provide all the 'information to make effective travel planning decisions', which translated means you can use it to check if your flight is delayed and you can have an extra hour at your desk/in bed/shopping for presents to bring home.

Registered members also have access to more detailed information including flight details, flight availability, mileage tracker and special discounts.

SPECIAL FEATURES

Find a Flight on the homepage is an amazingly speedy service. We selected a trip from Heathrow to Cape Town, chose a date and time, and within seconds two choices (British Airways and South African Airlines) appeared including details of flight time and type of aircraft. For booked flights, supply airline, flight number and date, and Check Flight Status will let you know just how long you might be twiddling your thumbs in the departure lounge.

Travel Essentials includes excellent destination details (including business hints and clothing as well as general country details), tips and features for businesses travellers, a directory of airline and airport website addresses, a mileage tracker (for consolidation of mileage and frequent flyer awards) and e-coupons travel discounts.

With OAG Mobile and FlightSync, OAG also provides flight status information to internet enabled mobile phones or palm pilots once you have registered your phone with one of the site's partners (AT&T and T-Motion). Sign up for OAG Mobile, and you can also have information emailed to you, or messages sent to a pager or mobile phone, no matter how you booked your flight.

An excellent resource and brilliantly swift – even if you use it just to find out who flies where and when.

www.btab.co.uk
Business Travel Connections

Overall rating: ★ ★ ★				
Classification:	travel agent	Readability:	★ ★ ★ ★	
Updating:	regularly	Content:	★ ★ ★ ★	
Navigation:	★ ★ ★ ★	Speed:	★ ★ ★ ★	

UK

A specialist business and corporate travel agent, and though the website contains sample information, the site directs you to phone or email the Southampton office. Service include flight reservations, car hire and accommodation, ticket delivery, passport and visa service, for Europe and the world, with the Middle East as a speciality.

SPECIAL FEATURES

Fares Samples gives you an idea of prices to a variety of cities, with a separate section for Middle Eastern destinations, and prices are given for business and economy class. The agency can offer special deals with Royal Jordanian Airlines.

Fact File gives details of a featured destination, with more countries covered 'on page 8' whose whereabouts is anyone's guess, but turns out to be under Useful Links. These cover the Foreign and Commonwealth Office, airports, embassies and visa information.

News has updates on airport developments, new destinations for airlines, for example, which could help frequent world hoppers.

The online presence of an offline travel agent, but with some good information.

travel information

www.a2btravel.com
Online Travel Corporation plc

Overall rating: ★ ★ ★ ★				
Classification:	Information	Readability:	★ ★ ★	
Updating:	regularly	Content:	★ ★ ★	
Navigation:	★ ★ ★ ★	Speed:	★ ★ ★	

UK R

Intended to be for holiday use on the whole, but as it also claims to be 'Britain's most comprehensive online travel resource', there should be much of use to the business traveller. Certainly the site is packed with information, brilliant links and online booking options here there and everywhere, but a2btravel somehow lacks the charm of Business Traveller (see p.122) and is certainly not as speedy. Minor irritations include a Loch Ness Monster icon which floats sedately across the page promoting Scotland.

SPECIAL FEATURES

Flight Booking Online is available, with links to UK airport and airline sites, and a link-up with www.travelocity.co.uk for booking flights with the best scheduled deals. There is also a fast track search facility for finding the published fares for all scheduled flights, though you need to register as a member for free use of this site after a couple of visits. The flight search is selected by best priced trips, and you supply date and time details, choice of class, number of connections and you can even specify your airline preference. Our hypothetical search for a Heathrow/New York JFK flight, with no particular airline, threw up nine options.

Insurance can be booked online through Green Flag.

Mapping, Currency, Weather contains the world-wide weather check (by city) comes via www.wunderground.com. The Currency section offers currencies at 0% commission, and free delivery when purchased online with a debit card.

Rail includes a2b's own phone line, but there is also a link to Railtrack's site, and online European rail timetables, including Eurostar.

Hotels, B&Bs, Villas lists 33,000 hotels, B&Bs and guests houses in the UK, selected by county or region (i.e. Cotswolds). You can search too by facilities, including conference facilities. The site's Hotel Booking Engine (link to OTC sister site) works by city selection world-wide, by date, hotel standard and particular requirements, and availability. The listings can be classified high rate to low or visa versa. The results show quickly with a 'more details' option button and discounts for booking online with OTC.

Car lists the best car rental deals, Shell's route planner and UK traffic News (from the RAC and Vauxhall Traffic Master) appear under the Car icon in the index.

Airport Parking can also be booked online, with substantial discounts available through the OTC sister site.

Jam-packed with information, there is lots here for those making their own business travel plans, but not for the business traveller per se and in some cases pretty slow to load.

www.biztraveler.org
Biztraveler

Overall rating: ★ ★ ★			
Classification:	Information	**Readability:**	★ ★ ★ ★
Updating:	occasionally	**Content:**	★ ★ ★ ★
Navigation:	★ ★ ★ ★	**Speed:**	★ ★ ★ ★
US			

A US site, the product of The National Business Travel Association, so much of the information is very American orientated, but its information, news and tips applies just as much to UK business travellers as US ones. The statistics on the amount of time one spends travelling are enough to have one scrambling to find advice on making it easier.

SPECIAL FEATURES

Road Rules has business traveller tips on all areas from air travel, to car rental, health and even women and travelling. The database of features is huge, and each area is split into general tips, news, travel tools, practices and policies and travel programmes, so click on the index on the right of the page which gives you an outline of the contents in each section.

Useable News deals with travel news and bulletins. Many are out of date and most US orientated, but more valuable is the Know Your Rights section, which provides airline luggage limits, customer rights by airline (all US) and who to contact when you have a complaint. Complaints are a key part of the site, and File A Complaint is the online opportunity to whinge about bad travel experiences. You can talk about almost any airline world-wide, and BizTraveler will forward your complaint to the relevant body.

International Travel has a currency converter and information about foreign entry requirements, plus Top 10

Tips for the International Business Traveller which apply to anyone.

OTHER FEATURES

If your business involves you spending hours gazing at the 'delayed' notice on the departures board of some international airport, take time to read the Soulful Traveler (sic) section. Here you'll find some advice on the art of airport relaxation: breath deeply and use airport waiting time creatively is the thrust of it.

There are travel safety alerts, all of which are horribly out of date by around a year, and the chance to participate in an online survey.

Some sound advice, and some entertainment, though we're not sure if it was meant that way.

www.businesstraveller.com
Business Traveller

Overall rating: ★ ★ ★ ★			
Classification:	magazine	Readability:	★ ★ ★ ★ ★
Updating:	regularly	Content:	★ ★ ★ ★ ★
Navigation:	★ ★ ★ ★ ★	Speed:	★ ★ ★ ★

UK

The online presence of the news-stand title, calling itself 'the one-stop shop for frequent business travellers'. The site provides airline and hotel reservations, up-to-the-minute travel news, guides to around 200 cities, expert travel advice, links to the websites of major airlines and hotel groups, and more.

Obviously a magazine specialising in business travel should be beyond reproach, and this enormous site earns top marks all round for being easy to follow, for thorough research and for its light, readable style. The index is broadly split into guides v news and magazine features.

SPECIAL FEATURES

City Guides are amongst the best we have found. Click on the area of the world map of interest, then on the city name. The information includes the best hotels (with a link to more) and places of interest all written in a down-to-earth way.

News is second to none in this specialist area. Covering car rental, airlines, hotels, airports and frequent flyers, there is up-to-date news on new routes, company branches, hotel chain expansion, discounts and special deals.

If you want links to airlines and hotel chains, look no further. Can there be an airline company it has missed out? If there is, it even asks you to let them know. The hotel guide works by map reference again, and is pretty strong on content, with details of room numbers, loyalty schemes and other essential information.

Essential Services is very good indeed, with a currency ordering online facility, currency converter, business travel insurance policies explained, a link to a mobile phone hire site, travel health, language learning, airport parking.

OTHER FEATURES

The features section of the magazine has a selection of tried and tested planes/hotels/train routes, written by the magazine's travel experts. There is no archive, and those featured are very recent. There is also the facility to ask the writers questions, and three or so previous Q&As appear on the questions page. The special offers are worth a look – it's not clear if these are exclusive to the magazine or not.

If you can't find the information here, you probably don't need to know it. The site leaves you with the feeling that business travel could almost be fun.

OTHER SITES OF INTEREST

British Airways Executive Club
www.britishairways.com/execclub
Part of the gargantuan BA website, The Executive Club is British Airways' frequent flyer programme, and you can earn miles when you fly on eligible fares with BA and partner airlines. Membership is at three levels and gives check-in benefits, use of special business lounges (with special facilities) amongst other privileges. Check the whole site map for all BA has to offer.

Expedia UK
www.expedia.msn.co.uk
Microsoft's booking site tailored to UK travellers, with a business section including flight timetable/car/hotel search, currency converter, Expedia information to your mobile service, and a link to bradmans.com, the destination information service for business people.

British Foreign and Commonwealth Office
www.fco.gov.uk/travel
Aimed at all British travellers, whether for business or pleasure, and full of sound advice. The country advice section works by selecting a country in the drop down menu, but also outlines countries not to be visited for any reason, or only for 'essential business purposes'. This information was last updated two months before we looked at the site. Select a country for travellers tips, and there is also an index of what to do if it all goes pear shaped.

Laptop Travel
www.laptoptravel.com
Here's a site for the twenty first century! Everything you ever needed to know about mobile computing, with product information on PDAs. wireless and laptops, technical support and wireless data services, and travel tips on hotel room connection, international net access and laptop security. A must for teccie business travellers.

Travel IQ
www.traveliq.co.uk
Travel IQ is a magazine specialising in business travel and tourism in Central and Eastern Europe and in the CIS. Most of the site is an advertisement for businesses to subscribe to the periodical, but some information available online is of use to businesses trading in that area of the world. Click on Inventory Quest for country profiles on certain Eastern European countries (though you will need to subscribe for a full list) and the Contacts link takes you to UK tour and travel operators and embassies and tourist boards in a directory searched alphabetically. Business Start-up is a long but informative article on where to go for advice on doing business for the first time in these areas of Europe, with links to sites such as Trade Partners UK and Business Link.

Virgin FlyinCo
www.virgin-atlantic.com
A relatively new idea from Virgin aimed at SMEs, but hard to find within the main site unless you go to the Search facility. Flyers can earn points towards the company's account and personal Flying Club miles. Privileges of membership include lounge passes, upgrades and limo transfers, free flights, car hire, and hotel accommodation. A questionnaire ascertains if you fit the suitable business criteria.

The Visa Service
www.visaservice.co.uk
London based service processing visa and passport applications for UK residents. Discount on handling fees for online customers.

World Executive Hotel Directory
www.worldexecutive.com
Simple to follow site with city guides to 75 major cities, with internet-only hotel offers, maps, weather and what to do. Hotels include details on meeting/conference facilities. There are also links to 3000 hotels world-wide searched by continent and city. Quick results and good details.

Railtrack
www.railtrack.co.uk
This is the main site of the Railtrack company, so provides information about rail safety, investor relations and industry partners. It's also the place to come for national timetable information. It' s very simple to use,and allows you to specify the time and date of travel, plus your chosen route. Click on the Details button for information on the type of train (express for example), and the operator, plus facilities on the train:.For fare information, you'll need to call or go to the specific train operators website. For these go to www.rail.co.uk which gives today's rail travel information from National Rail and a wonderful run down (with links) of all the national rail companies from Virgin to Merseyrail Electrics. The Travel Planner on this site takes you back to the Railtrack timetable details.

Business Travel About.com
http://businesstravel.about.com/mbody.htm
Part of the About.com portal phenomenon, which despite its US focus, features advice that is relevant whatever your nationality. This includes car rental problems and hints on avoiding the middle seat on an aircraft. There is plenty here for the UK business traveller, and there is even a link to the British Foreign and Commonwealth Office. The Airline Seat Maps on the long main index provides links to all major airline sites so you can book a specific place on the aircraft (though it doesn't say where the screaming child will be sitting). There are links too to the websites of all major worldwide airports, Asia business travel, banking and currency, city profiles, hotel chains and directories, travel insurance, weather, and sites for women business travellers.

Chapter 11

business sites for women

Though it sounds like positive discrimination to single out business sites aimed at women, there are too many of them to ignore. Statistics show that more than one million women run their own businesses in the UK; that is a third of all small businesses. By the very fact that there are sites aimed just for this section of the market, there must be a niche for them. But what do they have to offer?

One common theme seems to be enabling women to juggle careers with caring for children and family. Everywoman in particular aims to be a catch-all, covering subjects as diverse as tax advice and horoscopes. But although the site is valuable in itself, it's clear from the tone of many sites that business women do not want to be patronised and have cuticle care mixed with credit control. Many we found deal with the issues of women as entrepreneurs seriously and empathetically.

Several sites deal with networking, which especially attracts the many army of women who work from home or as sole traders. The frequency with which 'sold out' appears next to upcoming events organised by these network groups reveal that networking is popular; the testimonials show it to be effective.

Many of the network groups major on women and new technology. Women use the internet as often as men, but the attraction of these groups is that they offer training in a way angled towards women in the way women want to learn.

www.the-bag-lady.co.uk
The Bag Lady

Overall rating: ★ ★ ★ ★			
Classification: Information		**Readability:**	★ ★ ★ ★
Updating: regularly		**Content:**	★ ★ ★ ★
Navigation: ★ ★ ★		**Speed:**	★ ★ ★
UK			

Just over a year old, The Bag Lady is based in Wales and designed to promote women-owned businesses through an online directory, and to provide a forum for trading online, though this is still at the construction stage. There is also information about learning to do business on the Net, website reviews and general business information. Though its ideas are right on track, there is too much information packed onto the two centre columns of the home page, which makes it confusing to follow.

SPECIAL FEATURES

Trade Mall is still under construction, but promises to be a one year web-hosting facility for women business owners with a product or service to sell. Entries are at bronze, silver, gold and gold star levels which seems unnecessarily complicated.

Global Directory is searched by business type or business name, keywords and country and the choice of topics is wide. Featured businesses include email and website links, and business women can register their business for free.

Business One Stop Shop features an index of banks, associations, start-up and marketing sites, women's organisations, amongst a great number of others, and an interesting and supportive article about the stresses of being self-employed, which is written as much for men as women.

Links appears on the Technology page, flagged on the home page, where there is information to be found about UK technology initiatives and grants.

Forum had only just been launched, but promises web reviews and discussions on all aspects of business.

Despite the dubious name, The Bag Lady is full of good stuff. But like all good bag ladies, the information is disorganised. She could do with putting her house in order a bit.

www.bawe-uk.org
The British Association of Women Entrepeneurs

Overall rating: ★ ★ ★			
Classification:	networking	**Readability:**	★ ★ ★ ★
Updating:	regularly	**Content:**	★ ★ ★ ★
Navigation:	★ ★ ★ ★	**Speed:**	★ ★ ★ ★

UK   R

BAWE, a non-profit making professional organisation to promote the interests of UK-based women business owners, is nearly 50 years old. It is affiliated to the world association, Les Femmes Chefs d'Entreprises Mondiales, a member of The Confederation of British Industry, and works closely with the Department of Trade and Industry, the Institute of Directors, and the Chambers of Commerce. It works as a networking set up, with the opportunity for members to market and advertise on the site, join the BAWE WebRing, as well as organising trade missions and conferences around the world. The site is not registration only, and archived back issues of the Newsletter can be viewed online, but women need to register to join the organisation.

Not very dynamic as a web presence, but with barrels of experience behind it and strong international links, it's worth a look.

www.busygirl.co.uk
Busy Girl

Overall rating: ★ ★ ★ ★			
Classification:	information	**Readability:**	★ ★ ★ ★
Updating:	daily	**Content:**	★ ★ ★ ★
Navigation:	★ ★ ★ ★	**Speed:**	★ ★ ★ ★

UK

Despite the simply appalling name, which sounds more like a make-up tips site for coffee break time, Busy Girl comes as quite a surprise. It is a in fact a serious business technology network of over 4000 corporate and entrepreneurial women, sponsored by PricewaterhouseCoopers. Its aim is 'the economic advancement of women through business and career development', with corporate consultancy and business development services, and a monthly networking forum with a speaker at Pricewaterhouse Cooper's London Offices.

The site is split between Busy Girl Services and Community, with a survey featured on the home page ('Will women ever have equal representation in executive roles?') and business news items of the day searched via Ask Jeeves.

SPECIAL FEATURES

Busy Girl events and features, exclusive to the site include:

Networking Forums, which contains details of past speakers and information about booking up-coming events.

Web Design Training Courses, in association with New Horizons Computer Learning Centres, are engagingly explained, with 75 per cent discounts available to Busy Girl Club Members.

Services on the site include:

Women's Biz Directory allows you search for a women-owned business by category selecting the first letter or the industry. There are host of entries, with brief explanation, phone number and webpage link if applicable.

Women's Start-Up Info is more of an information resource explaining technology acronyms, or venture capital, emerging technologies or news-emails-to-your-desk services. The basics are not well covered.

Seeking Capital is a link to the SeekingCapital.com site, with discounts on its fund-finding services for Busy Girl members and Your Perfect Career is a link to justpeople.com, the online recruitment consultants.

The Busy Girl Community involves a discussion forum, newsletter and the opportunity to read profiles of other members, and to be profiled yourself.

Busy Girl is not the site to visit if you are starting up because the information in this section is not comprehensive enough. It is for women already established in technology-orientated businesses who want career support, and ideas for funding.

www.everywoman.co.uk
everywoman

Overall rating: ★ ★ ★ ★			
Classification:	Information	**Readability:**	★★★★
Updating:	regularly	**Content:**	★★★
Navigation:	★★★	**Speed:**	★★★★

UK   R

The UK version of the US site, Everywoman works hard to provide mainstream business information, and much geared towards women's interest in particular. Split into three areas, the site provides Business Resources, Workforce Information (Everywomen's online work option) and Home Support. Click on the drop down menu on the left of the page and choosing the area of interest. Business, for example, covers finance, law, networking, planning, resources and technology.

SPECIAL FEATURES

Workforce is a set up unique to Everywoman and put together in association with Ktopia, to create an online information service. The idea is to use 'online communities to provide cost effective solutions for collecting and creating content, evaluating the quality of information, and organising it to provide businesses with critical knowledge' or, in English, to provide a flexible option for women who can use their business skills and work online during the hours that suit them to contribute to market information available on the Internet.

Get Ahead in e-Business is a brief advert for the Start-up guide found on the Nat West Bank website (see p.36). Nat West has put together a basic feature about the importance of ecommerce in the market place. Written in association with Maxelon Consultancy, Streamline, WorldPay, Eversheds Solicitors and the University of Durham

Foundation for SME Development, the guide is split into six factsheets and is intended to help small businesses get online, get started in ecommerce, consider the key issues, make educated decisions and plans and set up and run a business website. The text is not especially aimed at women, and is well-written.

R&D Team is a business research area that requires registration. It may be free but access is not immediate, and you are contacted with your user name and password at a later date. This is frustrating if you need or want to view the pages immediately.

Ask Our Expert is a Q&A forum. You have to register on the site before you can email a question, but many of the more common topics are answered in the pages in the drop down menu on the left of the home page. The joining questionnaire is detailed to help Everywoman obtain a profile of the site's browsers. The Q&As are split between Business, which covers Tax Advice, Copyright and Intellectual Property Rights, Employment Law and Technology (with advice from IBM) amongst others, and Home which deals with Family Law and Personal Finance, as well as health issues like psychotherapy (from Jill Curtis at Family2000), fitness, diet and skincare. Click on the subject area for a CV of the experts featured. The names listed on the opening page are all women, but some men have crept in there too.

InfoBank is a novel name for the links page. Search by Business Association, or view the entire list which runs to 20 pages. The choice is impressive covering women's issues like abortion, the Muslim Women's Helpline, and the National Childbirth Trust as well as The Small Business Bureau and the Women Architects Committee of the RIBA.

OTHER FEATURES

The site tackles a vast array of subjects from horoscopes and relationships (with a link to Dating Direct.com), to a financial services page put together by Moneyextra.com. There's a link to the Wellbeing Channel and regular competition. Access to the bulletin forum is limited unless you register, but has useful exchanges of views on part-time work, good laptops and WAP phone information.

The selection of features, and number of experts on hand is excellent, but the InfoBank pages need special mention for the sheer breadth of subjects offered.

www.e-womenforum.com			
E-women Forum			
Overall rating: ★ ★ ★			
Classification: Network		**Readability:**	★ ★ ★ ★
Updating: regularly		**Content:**	★ ★ ★
Navigation: ★ ★ ★		**Speed:**	★ ★ ★ ★
UK R			

The recommendation here isn't so much for the site as for the cleverness of the idea. E-Women Forum is to support women working in new media, IT and ecommerce by providing monthly events for learning new skills, exchanging ideas and networking. The Forum also invites high profile speakers (Tracey Edwards MBE, Sonia Lo of eKoka Group to name but two) to talk on business issues in this emerging industry.

SPECIAL FEATURES

Forum   Join the forum and you receive information and newsletters, have the opportunity to join in events and share business information. Click under People in the left hand menu, and you can register to exchange skills and be in the suppliers' directory.

Learning Zone is a mixture of features and information supplied by members of the forum. Not all areas contain a feature, so it is not a comprehensive resource by any means, but there is some good stuff on marketing strategies for business ideas, and briefing a PR agency – much of this information gleaned from speakers' notes from E-Women Forum events.

The site itself is not very special, but it oozes with professionalism. For women working in this field, it is definitely one to look at.

www.ew-network.com			
EW-Network			
Overall rating: ★ ★ ★ ★			
Classification: Network		**Readability:**	★ ★ ★ ★ ★
Updating: regularly		**Content:**	★ ★ ★
Navigation: ★ ★ ★ ★		**Speed:**	★ ★ ★ ★
UK			

Another women-in-business networking site set up by Gwen Rhys, with a chatty, but professional feel to it (it promises 'no beauty tips, no fashion and no horoscopes'). Ew-Network has been around for over five years, holding Networking Forums around the UK and since 1997 has been holding Breakfast Briefings every month in London. Speakers are invited to talk at these meetings, and there is a chance to network with other associates. Information could only be found about the speaker for the next briefing, with dates only for subsequent ones.

Women can join at various levels of involvement, and the site also provides links to like-minded businesses women and their business services. Once you have subscribed to the site, you have the opportunity to share business tips online. The Useful Links page is not extensive, but carefully chosen.

This network does not provide any free information or business advice, but has a friendly and appealing tone. Would suit women who like the idea of no frills discussions about real business issues.

www.scottishbusinesswomen.co.uk

Scottish Business Women

Overall rating: ★ ★ ★ ★ ★			
Classification:	information	**Readability:**	★ ★ ★ ★ ★
Updating:	regularly	**Content:**	★ ★ ★ ★ ★
Navigation:	★ ★ ★ ★ ★	**Speed:**	★ ★ ★ ★

UK

Part of the Small Business gateway and Scottish Enterprise, this is an excellent site. It is simple to follow with only three main categories: news, information and community. The page design is appealingly uncomplicated, and the text written in this-is-how-it-is language. Though certain elements are aimed at Scottish Business in particular, there is just as much here for English, Welsh or Irish women too (if they don't mind us looking!)

SPECIAL FEATURES

News Section includes the opportunity to subscribe to the ezine newsletter, which covers a different subject each issue (this month cashflow). Back issues can also be viewed in the archive. The Business News index is good – select the story of interest flagged by its headline – and subjects covered include new legislation.

Information Pages are excellent, with a menu of business subjects to choose from and include business planning, legislation and regulations, ebusiness and finance. Under marketing, for example, there is one of the best features we have found on building a marketing strategy, with guidelines on advertising (who does what and when), direct mail, how to measure success and writing a marketing plan. Other areas covered in these pages include a link to www.wellpark.co.uk, the organisation for helping women in business (see p.132), very extensive FAQs, and a jargon buster (searched by keyword). Women's Resources provides links to organisations who carry out research into aspects of women's lives.

Community includes a discussion forum and a Member's Database for Scottish Businesses run by women. You can add your details or search by business category, keyword or letter. Find here too a link to www.businessmentoring scotland.org with information about how mentoring works.

What a shame this isn't a nation-wide site. It's kind on the eye and beautifully laid out with simple graphics and no bells and whistles. A very good source of information on business issues and worth bookmarking even if you live in Land's End.

OTHER SITES OF INTEREST

Business Friends
www.businessfriends.org
British women in business network organising informal meetings for exchanging business ideas. Membership only.

E-Command
www.e-command.co.uk
A networking site with events for people in marketing and new media.

DigitalEve
www.digitaleveuk.org
The UK 'Chapter' of the new global, non-profit making organisation for women in new media and digital technology. Started in the US, the UK site explains about monthly meetings for women wanting to learn about new technology. Organisation still under development.

National Association of Women Business Owners
www.nawbo.org
An American organisation affiliated to Les Femmes Chefs d'Entreprises Mondiales. Membership only but with some free-to-air articles.

Online Women's Business Centre
www.onlinewbc.gov
This is an American site, but there is useful information in Business Basics, including a strong list of business topics split into categories, including start up and funding advice, and Eleven Common Causes of Business Failure. Plenty here that applies to UK business, with an interesting feature on why women are good at small business.

Self-Employment
www.selfemployment.co.uk
Not strictly for women but an excellent online Resource Centre all the same, put together in association with Business Development Counsellor/Trainers from across the country who work through Enterprise Agencies. The site covers business planning and support, business information including regulations and marketing strategies, a pre-business checklist (tax, insurance, health and safety), and means for funding finance from grants to venture capital and loans. Well laid out and easy to follow.

Wellpark Enterprise Centre
www.wellpark.co.uk
All the details about the Glasgow-based information centre for Scottish women wanting to start their own business, and offering advice, counselling and training.

National Federation of Enterprise Agencies

www.smallbusinessadvice.org.uk is a web-based business support tool, conceived by the National Federation of Enterprise Agencies (NFEA). The service can be used by anyone wanting confidential free advice and guidance. If you have access to the Internet, you can post a business problem directly onto the NFEA's site. An appropriate Enterprise Agency adviser will then respond by e-mail direct to the enquirer.

www.smallbusinessadvice.org.uk is able to break down the traditional barriers to receiving support of time, location and mode of operation by enabling entrepreneurs to make an enquiry and receive information at their convenience through the Internet.

In addition to the enquiry service, the site also has chat rooms and discussion groups as well as providing useful links to other organisations.

NFEA is a network of independent, but not for profit, Local Enterprise Agencies. NFEA members offer advice and support to new and small businesses. In addition to support through the website, the NFEA can also put you in touch with your nearest Local Enterprise Agency. Details of all members and their services can be found on the NFEA's information site www.nfea.com.

Tel/Fax: 01234 354055
E-mail: enquiries@nfea.com
Websites:
www.nfea.com & www.smallbusinessadvice.org.uk

www.nfea.com

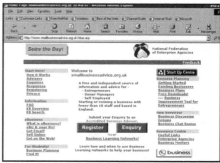

www.smallbusinessadvice.org.uk

Index